LUV

Murray Schisgal

WITH AN INTRODUCTION BY WALTER KERR
AND AN INTERVIEW WITH THE AUTHOR
BY IRA PECK

Coward-McCann, Inc.
New York

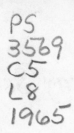

TITLE LETTERING BY NICHOLAS NAPPI

Second Impression

To REENE

INTRODUCTION
By WALTER KERR

I AM GOING to write 900 words on why I like Murray Schisgal.

I like Murray Schisgal because he is one step ahead of the avant-garde. The avant-garde, which is supposed to be ahead of everybody, has spent some years now scraping its aching feet against the dusty, inhospitable earth while standing in exactly the same place. Pick up a foot, put it down, move not at all but complain of the pain. The place where the avant-garde has been standing is known as The Brink. On the brink of despair, on the brink of the void, on the brink of a park-bench, the defeated have been observed waiting for Godot, waiting for love, waiting for a word that would make communication possible, waiting for someone or something to put them out of their misery. Occasionally they have tried to hang themselves from inadequate trees; sometimes they have succeeded in getting themselves disemboweled; mostly they have survived to disintegrate in the failing light, patient candidates for the trash-heap.

There has always been some aptness in the image: modern man does feel estranged and abandoned and all that. But there has often been something else in the image, especially as it began to repeat its nausea ad nauseam: there has been self-love, self-dramatization, romantic self-pity in it. See how drained I am, how devastated, the squirming near-cadaver says, proud of his position as The Man Who Has Been Most Badly Treated. The lower lip trembles but the eyes look up: where is that spotlight that will display me as victim? Come closer, spotlight; I have a very good speech ready about the abuse the silent universe has heaped upon me. The universe

Reprinted with permission from the New York Magazine of the New York Sunday Herald Tribune.

may be silent, but I will not be. Hear my moan. Isn't it something, really something, how I am ravaged?

I like Murray Schisgal because he hasn't stopped at this point, content to assume that we have come to the end of the line beyond which no bus runs and only ragweed grows. Mr. Schisgal doesn't necessarily deny that things are tough all over; he just sees how preposterous it is that we should take such *pleasure* in painting the clouds black.

If the avant-garde, up to now, has successfully exploded the bright balloons of cheap optimism, Mr. Schisgal is ready to put a pin to the soapy bubbles of cheap pessimism. Whatever social and philosophical stalemates we may have come to, wit at least need not be halted in its tracks. Wit may still venture forward. It may go right on to notice that the woe which has become so fashionable *is* fashionable; as such it is subject to some nose-thumbing. Wit may notice how thoroughly professionalized our postures of despair have become, how prepackaged our sorrows are, how slickly and sweetly the lozenges of lament roll about on our active tongues. Wit may look at the man who is trying to hang himself and say "Come off it."

That is one of the things Mr. Schisgal is doing in his new comedy, *Luv*, which I am happy to say looks like a very big hit. *Luv* is an extraordinarily funny evening in the theater, beautifully performed and maliciously directed, and I shouldn't be making it sound like *The Critique of Pure Reason*, even if it is quite plainly a criticism of fraudulent, opulent heartache. There is a park-bench in it, validating its avant-garde standing, upon which impassioned characters compare their unhappy childhoods, growing ever more furious at the thought that anyone, anywhere, might have been more maltreated, at nine, than they. There is a lamp-post in it, from which baggy-trousered Alan Arkin tries to hang himself after he has several times failed to leap from a bridge. Naturally he does not succeed; if he did he would have nothing to complain about. All three of the play's characters sooner or later pack knives. So does their author.

Mr. Schisgal's knife—it is a very sunny one, glinting brightly as it digs—is out for people who wear black on black while lovingly congratulating themselves upon the profundity of their losses. In the second act Anne Jackson turns up very smartly in black dress, black stockings, black boots, black raincoat. She couldn't be happier. Tragedies fill her life. She has been married twice, first to Eli Wallach and now to Mr. Arkin, which means that her capacity for suffering has been enormously enriched. "Now that I've lived with you," she confides with the deep, rolling throb of the old Roxy organ to Mr. Arkin, "I find you utterly obnoxious as a person." She doesn't say this unpleasantly; she says it *sincerely*. Nor does Mr. Arkin resent it. He listens, deeply sympathetic, then nods. "All right," he says, "that's a beginning." He understands the ground-rules of contemporary life, the shared horror upon which all secure relationships are founded. With luck, matters may get a good bit worse.

"I didn't ask for universal education, Harry. Why am I educated?" Miss Jackson cries in honest, succulent dismay. That is another of her tragedies. She knows so very, very much. And what she doesn't know she can easily make up, for she has read a great many books, including some with hard covers. She finally intuits, among other things, that Mr. Arkin is really in love with Mr. Wallach. Latent, of course. The spectacle of Mr. Arkin digesting this information, weighing its possibilities with a wary roll of his eyes, may just be the funniest single minute now available on Broadway. It is very difficult, you see, for any modern man to reject any suggestion that is sufficiently distressing. A fellow could be thought square, or could lose caste, if he denied out of hand a guilt he hadn't yet thought of.

As it happens, Mr. Arkin decides that this is one burden he does not care to take on. But it is about the only one. Knowledge has made nebishes of us all, and we had better learn how to comport ourselves as the *Angst* closes in. Miss Jackson does know how to comport herself. With an attitude on tap for every soul-searing occasion, she is now Phèdre fingering a cigarette, now Tallulah Bankhead caressing a growl, now any new-wave film heroine abandoning herself to existentialist necessity and the nearest male.

Because all human emotions are subject to ready analysis and readier revision—downwards, usually—there is some question whether any emotion dare be felt at all. Miss Jackson delivers Mr. Arkin a most serious blow. She announces that their new marriage is a failure. Mr. Arkin does not panic. After a moment of apparent paralysis, he simply crosses his legs comfortably and thinks about what he has heard. The question is: "Hmm. How shall I react *now?*"

Men do not live by bread or love alone, they live by affectation. Director Mike Nichols knows precisely how to display—in half a hundred zany visual images—the splendidly heartless disparity which has come to exist between the choked-up speeches we make and the frequently noticeable fact that we don't mean a word of them. Mr. Arkin dearly wishes to soothe his despairing friend Mr. Wallach, who is stretched out beating his fists against the floor of a bridge; he sits on Mr. Wallach while consoling him. Mr. Arkin is elated to hear that Miss Jackson loves him. He stamps violently on her foot and walks away. "Do you *still* love me?" he wants to know, sneakily, a moment later.

Due to the fact that our fashionable postures have become

detached from any actual processes that may be going on in our minds, passion—particularly anguish—can be applied to absolutely anything. "It was a cinnamon doughnut!" Mr. Wallach screams at one point, though we have no reason to believe that he has anything against cinnamon doughnuts. He simply needs one more injustice to charge against this miserably inconsiderate world.

I like Murray Schisgal because he has not only made his vision—that of Everyman wrapped in a cloak of borrowed pain—coherent, he has made it hilarious to begin with. Occasionally he settles for a merely constructed joke ("Do you know I'm more in love now than the day I married? But my wife won't give me a divorce") as occasionally, though very rarely, Mike Nichols stoops to the easy humor of producing chamber-pots. Ninety-nine per cent of the time author, actors, and director are occupied drawing brilliantly buoyant cartoons, antically animated, which do not have to struggle to Say Anything because they so perfectly contain—within their comedy—the "Come off it!" that lately needs to be said. An exaggerated drape of Miss Jackson's leg, or a Promethean lift of Mr. Wallach's chin, will do the trick. The spurious does not have to be explained when it is standing there, palpitating steadily, delighting us in the very overripeness of its stance.

I see that I have gone beyond 900 words, but then I liked Anne Jackson, Eli Wallach, and Alan Arkin, too.

AN INTERVIEW WITH THE AUTHOR
By IRA PECK

JUDGING from the sinuous lines winding from the box office of the Booth Theater on Shubert Alley, the town's newest comedy "smash" is a three-character play that goes under the heading of a three-letter non-word called *Luv*.

An impudent comedy, it spoofs, among other things, love, marriage, self-pity, despair, suicide, and homosexuality. Sometimes it suggests Luigi Pirandello, sometimes James Thurber; it has moments when it is pure Marx Brothers. Yet it is uniquely the work of Murray Schisgal, a 37-year-old son of a clothes presser from East New York in Brooklyn, who, until *Luv*, was known only for a pair of one-act plays presented off Broadway, *The Typists and The Tiger*.

Mr. Schisgal's current abode is a modestly furnished apartment (without television) on West End Avenue where he lives with his wife, Reene, and their eight-month-old daughter, Jane. A bearded, rather sad-faced man with heavy eyelids, he favors comfortable, unassuming sports clothes.

How had he taken to his new-found success?

"I still haven't digested it," he replied. "It means nothing to me yet primarily because I haven't gotten a check. I'm not doing anything different today (Friday, two days after *Luv* had opened) than I was doing Monday. I know that when *The Typists and The Tiger* were done I promised to have my teeth fixed. They were a success and I did. Now that my teeth are fixed, I want to go out and buy some shoes and some pants and a velour hat which I saw on Fifth Avenue the other day and I'll probably—" Mr. Schisgal came to a halt. "What else can I get? I'm not going to move, I don't want a car, I'm not going away. I don't know. It's a problem, isn't it?"

We remarked to Mr. Schisgal that as we were leaving a recent performance of *Luv* we overheard a woman say that though she had enjoyed the play hugely, she wasn't sure she knew what it meant. Would he care to enlighten her?

Mr. Schisgal (the accent is on the second syllable) seemed unhappy with the question.

"The theater is an experience," he said. "To have that experience is to participate in a theatrical event. There is no reason that I know of why experience need be the answer to a question, the narration of a story, or a statement about reality. Why do people want everything tied up in a neat little homily? Why must they be able to say, 'This means ta *ta* ta ta *ta* ta ta ta ta ta ta.' This is particularly bad because it excludes from the theater a vitality and a sense of the wonderful which of necessity is ambiguous and escapes clear-cut definition.

"If you look at a modern painting today, how silly it would be to say, 'I don't know what it means.' The question should be, 'What am I experiencing? What is delighting me? What are my own feelings in relationship to it?' That's what I think the theatergoer owes to himself to go to the theater for—not for answers, but for experience. Otherwise, they're excluding from themselves something that can be more meaningful than answers."

Nevertheless, Mr. Schisgal ventured a few words about the meaning of *Luv*.

"The sense of it is that the emotion of love has been perverted and misused to such an extent that it can only be defined by using another word which comes closer to what we experience, to what we think, and how we behave. It can be l-u-v, l-o-v, or x-y-z, but it certainly can't be a word that has been abused as much as l-o-v-e. L-u-v is the perversion of l-o-v-e. I don't have the audacity to define the other."

In what sense did he feel that love has been abused or perverted?

"In the sense that we use it as a repository for insincerity, for physical desire, and perhaps primarily for money. I'm thinking of the cheap movies, the cheap books, and the cheap slap-dash psychological tripe that is continually being drummed into our heads.

"It becomes increasingly apparent that there is financial value in perverting human emotion to suit adolescent fancy and it is this perversion that is sold to the gullible and to which we ourselves are exposed at an age of non-discretion that proves so harmful when we are called upon to behave as adults.

"Love has become a commodity rather than an emotion. By a commodity I mean relationships. By pretending in personal relationships that what we say is what we mean. To talk so glibly that our words are removed from our feelings. To be so 'hip' that we don't even know what our feelings are."

Considering the despair voiced by the three characters in his play, what are his own views of life?

Mr. Schisgal thought it over a few moments before answering.

"I'm trying to make a living, I'm trying to do the work that I think I am suited for, and my attitude towards life is the result of the multitude of experiences I've had, very few of which I fully comprehend. I know of no conclusions about anything and I don't have answers and I don't think it is my work to be concerned with them. My work is to write about those things which impinge upon me and which for whatever reason demand to be put down on paper."

How did *Luv* evolve?

"There are no doubt playwrights who write plays from ideas or premises," Mr. Schisgal replied. "To date I have written plays from characters. Out of characters evolve the ideas. The three characters in *Luv* had been sitting in my head for a good number of years and, for no apparent reason, one day they just stood up and started shouting at me. They're composites of people I've known but no one is any one person."

How much of the almost wildly comic effect of *Luv* did he attribute to the play itself and how much to the direction of Mike Nichols and the actors?

"I worked very closely with the actors and the director from the first day of rehearsal," he replied. "I don't think I will ever tire of saying that the contribution of the director and the actors equalled my own.

"A production is not a play. A production is the involvement of several people having in common a single vision. It was my very good fortune here to be working with people who didn't deny that vision but aided and abetted it. I guess I have to thank Claire Nichtern, the producer, because her desire to see the play done as I envisioned it was as strong as anyone else's."

Mr. Schisgal has been writing ever since he was 21. But until he turned to drama a few years ago with *The Typists and The Tiger*, he had been notably unsuccessful. His output had included some 60 short stories and three novels, none of which were published. "They were all quite bad," he said.

To support himself during this period, Mr. Schisgal worked at an astonishing number of odd jobs including setting up pins in a bowling alley, playing in a band, hanging up dresses in Klein's, and pushing a hand truck in the garment center.

"My primary concern was to find time and a place to write," he said. "It was never with school or with the job I had at the time."

Most of Mr. Schisgal's education was obtained at night, at

Long Island University, Brooklyn Law School, and the New School for Social Research. Mr. Schisgal practiced law for two years in an office on Delancey Street but gave it up when he found it was taking too much time and attention from his writing. Then he took up teaching.

It was while teaching English at the James Fenimore Cooper Junior High School in East Harlem that he decided to turn to drama.

"I don't believe it was brought about by design," he said. "I didn't sit down one day and say, 'I'm a dramatist.' The last novel I was working on wasn't going any place and I imagine that primarily out of frustration I started writing plays."

He turned out five one-act plays, two of which were *The Typists and The Tiger*. He was on his way to Spain via London "to do nothing but write" when a friend suggested that the British Drama League might be interested in his plays. That's how *The Typists and The Tiger* came to be produced in London, initiating Mr. Schisgal into the theater. Later they were produced off Broadway starring Eli Wallach and Anne Jackson, who also star in *Luv*.

Currently Mr. Schisgal has completed two new plays *Ducks and Lovers* and *Jimmy Shine* but he is reluctant to discuss them.

"I much prefer for people to discover the sense of the play when it's produced rather than being keyed in beforehand," he said.

Would he say that the turning point in his life came when he decided to try drama?

"I'd be a joker if I said differently," Mr. Schisgal replied. "If nothing else I seem to be making a living at it—and perhaps that's not a bad thing."

Luv
opened in New York,
November 12, 1964,
at the Booth Theatre
with the following
cast:

CHARACTERS
(In order of appearance)

Harry Berlin	*Alan Arkin*
Milt Manville	*Eli Wallach*
Ellen Manville	*Anne Jackson*

Luv was presented by Claire Nichtern
Directed by Mike Nichols
Designed by Oliver Smith
Lighting by Jean Rosenthal
Costumes by Theoni V. Aldredge
Music for song by Irving Joseph

ACT ONE

THE TIME:
The Present: evening.

THE SCENE:
A bridge. The railing of the bridge crosses, rear, at an angle: it is interrupted on the left by a small boxlike alcove, then continues; swooping above and disappearing out of sight on the right is a thick red coil from which cables descend at regular intervals and connect to the railing. Two wooden slab-boarded benches, placed back to back, one facing downstage, the other upstage, are at the right, also at an angle. Farther on the right is an old iron-cast lamppost, which is lit. On the left, forward, is a nondescript unmarked sandbox, no larger in size than three orange crates lying side by side. Farther left, forward, is a public wire-mesh trash basket. A curbstone cuts across the front at an angle and the entire stage is raked.

The faint sounds of a foghorn, a motor churning in the water, a buoy bell, etc.

HARRY BERLIN (*tall, flabby, with a bristly mustache, in ill-fitting rumpled clothes: a threadbare dark-green corduroy jacket, an open-necked faded blue work shirt, no tie, very large khaki pants tied to his waist by a string, dirty white tennis sneakers*) *leans on the railing in the alcove, rear, facing upstage, and stares at the river below.* MILT MANVILLE (*thin, erect, of less than average height, in a sharply tailored "continental" brown suit,*

*pink shirt with rolled collar, bright yellow tie
and pocket handkerchief, large cuff links, and
brown suede shoes) enters, left, paces up and
down, looks at his watch anxiously; his eye soon
falls on the trash basket; he is drawn irresistibly
toward it; he bends over and examines a worn
discarded velvet-collared gray herringbone overcoat.*

HARRY *turns.* MILT *notices him, stares forward,
trying to recall where he has seen him before.*
HARRY *takes pad, pencil from pocket, writes a
note, slaps it on railing; he drops his jacket to
ground and climbs up on railing.*

MILT. (*With a sense of recognition, moving up to him*) Is
it . . .
        HARRY *turns, stares down at him.*
No, Harry Berlin! I thought so! I just caught a glimpse of
you and I said to myself, "I bet that's Harry Berlin. I just
bet that's Harry Berlin." And sure enough, it's old Harry
Berlin himself.
        Taking HARRY's *hand; shaking it.*
How have you been doing, Harry? What's been happening?
        HARRY *squats and slowly comes down from rail-
ing.*
It must be . . . why, at least fifteen years since I saw you
last. We had that party after graduation, I said, "Keep in
touch," you said, "I'll call you in a few days," and that's
the last I heard of you. Fifteen years.

HARRY. (*Feigning recognition*) Is it fifteen years?

MILT. Fifteen years.

HARRY. Hard to believe.

MILT. Fifteen years next month as a matter of fact.

HARRY. Time sure flies.

MILT. It sure does.

HARRY. Fifteen years next month.

MILT. Fifteen years.

HARRY. (*Slight pause*) Who are you?

MILT. Milt! Milt Manville! Your old classmate at Polyarts U.

HARRY. (*Grabbing his hand*) That's right! Milt! Milt Manville!

> *They embrace; laugh joyfully.* HARRY *puts on jacket, then crumples note, throws it over railing as* MILT *speaks.*

MILT. Say, Harry, I've been doing wonderful for myself; terrific. Got into the brokerage business during the day: stocks, bonds, securities, you know. The money's just pouring in; doing fabulous. Got into secondhand bric-a-brac and personal accessories at night: on my own, great racket, easy buck. And, say, I got myself married. Oh yeah, I went and did it, finally did it. Ellen. A wonderful, wonderful girl. Do anything for her. A home in the suburbs, no kidding, thirty-five thousand, and that's not counting the trees, big tremendous trees; you should see them. Hey. Look at this watch. Solid gold. Twenty-two carats.

> *Opening his jacket to reveal garish yellow lining.*

Notice the label?

> *Unbuttons shirt.*

Silk underwear. Imported. Isn't that something?

> *Lifts arm.*

Hey, smell this, go ahead, smell it.

> HARRY *is reluctant to come too close;* MILT *presses his head to his armpit; laughing.*

Not bad, huh?

> *Solemnly.*

Well, how's it been going, Harry? Let's hear.

HARRY. (*Mournfully*) Awful, Milt; awful. It couldn't be worse. I'm at the end of the line. Everything's falling apart.

MILT. (*Perplexed*) I don't get it.

HARRY. The world, Milt. People. Life. Death. The old questions. I'm choked with them.

MILT. (*Still perplexed*) Oh.

HARRY. (*Arm around him, leads him forward right*) I must have been out of school for only a couple of weeks when . . . it happened. Out of the blue. Disillusionment. Despair. Debilitation. The works. It hit me all at once.

MILT. Oh. Ohhhh.

> HARRY *sits on curbstone.* MILT *puts down white handkerchief, sits beside him.*

HARRY. I remember . . . I was sitting in the park. It was Sunday, a hot lazy Sunday. The sun was burning on the back of my neck. An open book was on my lap and I was kind of daydreaming, thinking of the future, my plans, my prospects . . . Then . . . Suddenly . . . Suddenly I looked up and I saw, standing there in front of me . . . How can I put it in words? It was a dog, Milt. A fox terrier. I'd swear it was a fox terrier. But who knows, I . . .

MILT. (*Interrupting*) Let's just say it was a dog, Harry.

HARRY. It was a dog. Right.

MILT. A dog. Go ahead.

[6

HARRY. And . . . And he was there, right in front of me, standing on his hind legs and . . . He looked almost like a little old man with a little white beard and a little wrinkled face. The thing is . . . Milt, he was laughing. He was laughing as loudly and as clearly as I'm talking to you now. I sat there. I couldn't move. I couldn't believe what was happening. And then, he came up to me, now he was walking on all fours and . . . When he got up to me . . . When he got up to me, he raised his leg and . . .

MILT. No.

HARRY. (*Nodding, with twisted expression*) All over my gabardine pants. And they were wet, through and through. I could swear to that! Then he turned right around and walked off. The whole thing was . . . It was all so unreal, all so damn senseless. My mind . . . I thought . . .
    Emotionally.
Why me? Out of everyone in that park, out of hundreds, thousands of people, why me?
    MILT *looks about bewilderedly.*
What did it mean? How do you explain it?
    In control of himself.
That started it; right there was the beginning. From that minute on, it changed, everything changed for me. It was as if I was dragged to the edge of the cliff and forced to look down. How can I make you understand? What words do I use? I was nauseous, Milt. Sick to my soul. I became aware . . . aware of the whole rotten senseless stinking deal. Nothing mattered to me after that. Nothing.

MILT. Your plans to go to medical school?

HARRY. I couldn't.

MILT. The book you were writing?

HARRY. (*Throwing up his hands*) No use.

MILT. Your Greek studies?

HARRY. I couldn't. I couldn't go on.

> *Rises; moves to sandbox, paces around it;* MILT *also rises.*

No roots. No *modus vivendi*. I had to find some answers first. A reason. I traveled, went everywhere, looked everyplace. I studied with a Brahmin in Calcutta, with a Buddhist in Nagoya, with a Rabbi in Los Angeles. Nothing. I could find nothing. I didn't know where to turn, what to do with myself. I began drinking, gambling, living in whorehouses, smoking marijuana, taking guitar lessons . . . Nothing. Still nothing. Tonight . . . Milt, tonight I was going to end it all, make one last stupid gesture of disgust and . . . that would be it!

MILT. (*Glances at railing*) You don't mean . . .

HARRY. That's right.

MILT. (*Going to him*) How terrible. How terrible, Harry. I'm ashamed of you at this minute. I'm ashamed to have been your classmate at Polyarts U.

HARRY. Ask me what I believe in, Milt.

MILT. What do you believe in, Harry?

HARRY. I believe in nothing, Milt.

MILT. Nothing? That's terrible. How can someone go on living without believing in anything?

HARRY. That's the problem I'm faced with. And there's no answer to it, none, except down there!

> *He points to railing, moving to bench.*

MILT. (*Turns* HARRY *toward him*) Now let's not lose our heads. Let's control ourselves. Keep calm. Keep calm. Now listen to me. I can understand. I can understand everything you said, but, Harry . . . Don't you think it's more than unusual, just a little more than unusual, that I happened to be passing at the very minute, the precise exact minute, that you were contemplating this . . . this horrible thing?

HARRY. (*Pointing upward*) You don't mean . . . ?

MILT. (*Throwing both hands up defensively*) I'm not saying it! I didn't say it!
Wagging finger.
But just remember, science doesn't have all the answers!

HARRY. Talking about it only makes it worse, Milt. You don't know what agony I've been through. It's gotten so bad that sometimes, sometimes, in the middle of the day or night, without a warning of any kind, my whole body becomes paralyzed, I can't move a muscle and . . .
In mid-speech his body stiffens like a board and he topples forward. MILT *catches him at the last moment, shouts and shakes him frantically.*

MILT. Harry! What is it? Harry, for God's sake . . .
He runs around in a complete circle, holding HARRY *whose stiff body revolves like the hand of a clock.*
Help! Help! Help, here! Help! Help!
To HARRY.
Look at me! Speak to me, Harry!

HARRY. (*Calmly*) That's the way it happens.

MILT. (*Sitting on sandbox*) You scared the life out of me. That's terrible. Why don't you see a doctor, a specialist, someone . . .

HARRY. I don't have to see anyone. I know what it is, Milt.

The will to live drops out of me, plops right out of me.
Why move? I say to myself. Why do anything? But that's
not all of it. Sometimes, sometimes, I can't see, I lose the
power of sight completely and I grope about . . .
> *Throws up his hands, feigns blindness and moves
> dangerously close to the edge of the stage.*

Milt . . . Milt . . . Where are you? Are you still here,
Milt?

MILT. (*Jumps up, grabs him in the nick of time*) Right here,
Harry. I'm right here.

HARRY. (*Clawing behind him at* MILT's *face*) Help me, Milt.
Help me get to the bench.

MILT. (*Pushing him forward*) Of course. This way, Harry.
That's it. Watch your step. Here, here it is.
> *They're seated on bench.*

HARRY. (*Calmly*) Thank you, Milt.

MILT. Is there . . . anything else I can do?

HARRY. No. I'm all right now. That's the way it happens.

MILT. I would never have believed it.

HARRY. Why see? I say to myself. Why be a witness to it?
> *Grabbing* MILT's *lapels.*

Why, Milt? Why?

MILT. I don't know, Harry. I don't know.
> *Pulling himself free; straightens tie, etc.*

HARRY. So I go blind and I don't see. The whole thing becomes completely automatic. I have no control over it.

MILT. But there must be something you can do.

HARRY. (*Cupping hand to ear, feigns deafness; loudly*) What
did you say, Milt?

MILT. I said, "There must be something you can do to correct . . ."

HARRY. I can't hear you, Milt. Speak slowly and I'll try to read your lips.

MILT. (*Speaking slowly, loudly, drawing out words*) I said, "There must be something you can do to . . ."

HARRY. (*Abruptly; calmly*) I hear you now, Milt. That's another one of my . . . my fits. Sound becomes so damn painful to me . . . Why listen? I say to myself. Why listen?

MILT. Incredible. I wouldn't have believed it was possible.

HARRY. Well, it is. Look at me. I'm a living example of it. Now you can . . .

> He feigns muteness, his mouth opening wide and closing without uttering a sound; gesturing.

MILT. (*Becoming increasingly distraught*) Harry? Are you speaking to me, Harry? Harry, I can't hear you. Can you speak . . .

> HARRY removes pad and pencil from jacket pocket, jots something on pad.

Oh, God, not that, too.

> Glances at HARRY's note.

I understand, Harry. I . . . Give me that.

> Takes pencil and pad from HARRY; he starts writing.

"Dear Harry, What we have to keep in mind, no matter what . . ."

> HARRY pulls pencil out of MILT's hand. MILT pulls it away from HARRY.

MILT. (*Angrily*) The least you can do is let me finish!

> Starts writing again.

HARRY. I can hear you, Milt.

MILT. You can?

HARRY. I can't speak when that happens, but I hear all right. Why speak? I say to myself. Words have no meaning; not anymore. They're like pebbles bouncing in an empty tin can.

MILT. (*Pockets pad, pencil*) I don't know what to say, Harry.

HARRY. What can you say? It's no good, Milt; no good. For cryin' out loud, let me get it over with!

> *Removes rope with noose from jacket pocket as he speaks, puts noose over his head and after throwing rope over crossbar on lamppost, tries to hang himself by pulling on end of rope.*

MILT. (*Rises*) No, no! Harry! Harry, will you listen to me? *Slapping at his hands.*
Let go! Let go of it!

> *HARRY slumps to foot of lamppost where he sits dejectedly.*

There's plenty of time for that!

> *He takes rope from lamppost and at the same time releases pin from crossbar so that it can swing.*

Did it ever occur to you that you're in the state you're in because you've never known the feeling that comes with money, with power, with influence?

HARRY. (*Removes noose from his neck; disparagingly*) Ahhh, Milt . . .

MILT. (*Rolling rope together*) Now don't brush it aside. Look at me, Harry, and ask yourself, "Why did he go up so high and I go down so low?" Ask yourself that.

> *Moves to trash basket.*

We both started out on the same foot; as a matter of fact you started out ahead of me, you had the money your folks left you. I had nothing but my two hands and a quick eye. When other people slept, I worked. When other people said it couldn't be done, I went out and did it.

> *He lifts worn velvet-collared herringbone overcoat out of basket—it is buttoned; he ties collar with rope, making a bag of it.*

And through diligence, self-confidence, perseverance, I've made something of myself!

HARRY. (*Rises*) My folks left me a few stinking thousands, that's true, but don't you forget I never lived with them, I was brought up by my grandparents, and it was hell, believe me, it was hell.

MILT. (*Drops overcoat to ground*) Ha! You should have lived with my folks for a couple of weeks, then you would have known what hell is really like. Those two were like a pair of cats at each other's throat. And the poverty, the lousy humiliating poverty. I didn't start school until I was eight years old because I didn't have a pair of shoes to wear. Oh, yeah. Lucky for me the kid downstairs was hit by an ice-cream truck and I got his shoes. Even then they were so tight on me I couldn't walk. I was put in a special class for disabled children.

HARRY. You think that was bad? My grandparents used to lock me out of the house. They couldn't stand the sight of me because I reminded them of my father. I remember one day I came home from school during a blinding snowstorm and the door was locked. I knocked and yelled and beat my poor little frozen fists on the door . . . They laughed at me. They laughed! Picture that for yourself. A tall skinny kid standing out there in the snowstorm, wearing nothing but a thin torn jacket and a paper bag for a hat, knocking and yelling, "Let me in. Please, let me in!"

MILT. Paradise.

> *Slight pause.*

It was paradise compared to my childhood. Picture this. It's late at night. The wind's blowing outside. A small undernourished boy sits by the cold kerosene stove, feeding his toy wooden horse a bit of bread that he stole during dinner. The parents are quarreling. "If you don't like it here, get the hell out," the father shouts. "You're telling me to get out," the mother shouts back, and with savage hysterical fury she picks up the boy's toy wooden horse and throws it at the father. He ducks and it smashes against the wall. The boy drops down beside his broken toy horse, the only thing he ever loved, and he cries quietly.

HARRY. (*Moves right, then whirls back to* MILT; *pugnaciously*) Did you ever get beaten?

MILT. (*Emphatically*) I did.

HARRY. With what?

MILT. A strap, a stick, a radiator cover.

HARRY. A chain?

MILT. How thick?

HARRY. As thick as my wrist.

MILT. (*Foiled; moves away, turns*) What did you get for breakfast?

HARRY. At home?

MILT. At home.

HARRY. A glass filled with two-thirds water and one-third milk.

[14

MILT: Coffee grounds, that's what I got.

HARRY. With sugar?

MILT. Not on your life. I ate it straight, like oatmeal.

HARRY. (*Foiled; moves away, suddenly turns*) Did your mother ever kiss you?

MILT. Once. When I stuck my head between her lips and a picture of Clark Gable.

HARRY. Well, that's better than I did.

MILT. (*Foiled; moves about*) What presents did you get for Christmas?

HARRY. Presents? When I was five my grandparents bought a box of doughnuts and every Christmas until I was seventeen I got a doughnut.

MILT. You were a lucky kid and you didn't know it.

HARRY. (*Bawling*) They were cinnamon doughnuts!

MILT. Harry, you're missing the whole point. Even if we started out on the same foot, I went ahead and became a success, I pulled myself up to a position of responsibility, of respect, of importance. And don't think it was easy. It was dog-eat-dog all the way.

> *Picks up overcoat, puts wine bottle, magazine into it.*

But I stuck with it, gave it all I had, worked at two jobs, stocks, bonds, securities during the day, secondhand bric-a-brac and personal accessories at night.

> *Takes naked doll from trash basket, waves it in air before inserting it into overcoat.*

Rain or shine, sick or well, seven days a week, fifty-two weeks a year. I never let up, not even after I had achieved

15]

what I had set out to do. Right to the top. On my own. Every inch of the way.

> *Removes baby's chamber pot from trash basket, turns it in his hand before dropping it into overcoat.*

And let me tell you, Harry, nothing, nothing succeeds like success.

> *He ties bottom of overcoat with rope.*

HARRY. You know I'm not interested in any of that, Milt. I need something else to go on. A *Weltanschauung*. A reason for living. That isn't easy to come by, either.

> *He moves to curbstone, right.*

Everything I taste turns sour in my mouth. Everything I touch becomes dust in my hands. It's as if I was standing at the bottom of the world and all I'd have to do is sit down to be dead.

> *He sits down on curbstone.*

MILT. (*Leaving overcoat on ground, moves to him*) Stop talking like that. How could you have changed so much? I still can't believe it. At school you were one of the boys, full of life, ready for a laugh and a good time at the drop of a hat.

> *Squatting behind him, holding his shoulder and pointing out into the distance.*

Remember, Harry, remember our marching down the football field in our red and gold uniforms, you leading the Polyarts All-Girl Band on the right, with me leading them on the left, our batons twirling in the air . . .

> *He rises, struts up and down the bridge, singing, twirling an imaginary baton—he throws it up, catches it, kicks it with the heel of his shoe, catches it, performs tricks of this sort.*

Alma mater, alma mater,
Forward to the fray;
We will win our victory,
And move right on our wa-a-a-a-ay.

> HARRY *nods, mumbles,* "Yes, yes, I remember,
> yes, yes . . ."

Alma mater, alma mater,
Lift your light up high;
We will win our victory,
And come back by and by.

Da, da, da, da, da, da, da . . .

HARRY. (*Rises, breaking spell of past with an anguished shout*)
It's no use, Milt. Cut it out. It only makes it worse!

> MILT *slumps on bench, panting heavily.*

(*Pacing*) You're right, though. At school everything was
different. I was different. I expected so much . . . From
myself. From the world. From the stars, the sun . . . Do
you remember what they used to call me at school?

MILT. (*Humbly*) Dostoyevski.

HARRY. That's right. Dostoyevski. What ambition I had.
What energy. My medical career, my writings, my Greek
studies . . . Always had my nose in a book, always scrib-
bling things down, projects, plans, new ideas, new fields to
investigate, to explore . . .

> His voice dwindles to a wail; he suddenly pulls
> off jacket, throws it to ground.

Let me do it now and be done with it!

> He climbs onto railing.

MILT. (*Runs after him*) Harry! Harry!

> HARRY *covers his face with his hands, screams and*
> *jumps off the railing, landing to his stunned sur-*

17]

prise on the bridge; he turns and rushes back to
railing. MILT *grabs him, throws him down to*
ground.

MILT. Listen to me a minute. This is terrible, terrible. That
you should treat life so cheaply . . . It's a sin! There.
He boots him in the backside.
I said it and I'm glad!
Contemptuously.
Look at you. At your age, worn out, defeated, wrecked in
body and soul. It takes guts to go on living, Harry. It takes
guts to make something of your life.
From behind he holds HARRY *under his arms and*
lifts him to a sitting position; softer tone.
Harry, listen to me. Love . . .

HARRY. Love?

MILT. (*Taking chin in his hand*) Yes, Harry. Love, human
love, the love of a small boy for his toy wooden horse, the
love of an old classmate, the love of a man for a woman.
Doesn't that mean anything to you?

HARRY. What do you think's been keeping me going this long?
He rises, moves left, forward.

MILT. (*Rises*) Well?

HARRY. I don't know if I can love, Milt.

MILT. That's what everyone says until they meet the right
woman. And then . . .

HARRY. What?

MILT. You don't know?

HARRY. How could I?

MILT. You don't mean . . . ?

HARRY. (*Shaking his head; mournfully*) Not once.

MILT. Oh, Harry. Harry, to have lived and not have loved
. . . Do you call that living?
Stepping on sandbox.
You don't know what life is, how can you destroy it?

HARRY. (*Moving right to lamppost. Picks up jacket on way*)
Love. We read about it, all right; we hear a lot about it.
But where is it, Milt? Where? I haven't seen it and I've
been through the mill and around the world twice.
Puts jacket on bench.

MILT. (*Moving to him*) It's because your eyes are closed,
Harry; your eyes are closed. Do you think I could go on,
working day after day, giving my youth, my health, my life
itself, for a handful of shekels, for a few clammy coins, if
there wasn't some compensation for it, something that
made it all worthwhile?

HARRY. You do understand.

MILT. Of course I understand. Ask me what I believe in,
Harry.

HARRY. What do you believe in, Milt?

MILT. I believe in love, Harry.

HARRY. Love?

MILT. Love!

HARRY. If I thought there was a chance . . .

MILT. Of course there's a chance. Being alive gives you that
chance. And now that we've met . . . I'll help you, Harry;
introduce you to people, show you around. You'll meet
some woman and, boy, let me tell you, one day you'll get
down on your knees and thank me. What do you say?

HARRY. I don't know how I'm going . . . You have to understand . . .

> *Turns away from him.*

It's not easy . . . Life . . . The stars . . . The sun . . .
I . . .

> *He suddenly stiffens and falls backward like a pole; MILT catches him, prevents him from falling to ground.*

MILT. Harry! Harry! Don't start that again!

> *MILT sits on bench, holding HARRY's stiff body.*

For God's sake. Harry . . . Love.

> *Shouts in his ear.*

Love!

HARRY. (*His body relaxing, he slides between MILT's legs*) It . . . It did it, Milt. It worked. I swear.

> *Rises.*

As soon as you said the word love, I felt my whole body begin to melt and I . . . I suddenly felt . . .

MILT. (*Rises*) You see? What did I tell you? Give it a chance.

HARRY. (*Enthusiastically*) Give love a chance.

MILT. Why not?

HARRY. I have nothing to lose.

MILT. What can you lose?

HARRY. (*Pointing to rail*) I can . . . always end things if I want.

MILT. (*Repeating his gesture*) Of course you can.

HARRY. All right, Milt.

MILT. (*Retrieves jacket, puts it on HARRY, buttons it*) That's my old schoolbuddy. Now you promise . . .

HARRY. You have my word on it.

MILT. No more of this foolishness.

HARRY. (*Sits on bench*) No more.

MILT. Wonderful. Wonderful.
> *Sits beside him.*

There's nothing in the world like it, Harry. It's like getting a new lease on life; it changes everything; one minute you're down in the gutter, the next you're up in the clouds. Do you know I'm more in love today than on the day I married.

HARRY. You don't mean . . . ?

MILT. That's right. But my wife won't give me a divorce.
> *Rises.*

She's a wonderful woman, Harry; don't get me wrong. I'd do anything for her. But once love goes, what's left? There's no thrill to it, no excitement, no surprises . . . Look, here's her picture.
> *Takes out wallet-photograph.*

HARRY. Your wife?

MILT. No, no, the girl I want to marry. Linda. Isn't she beautiful? Everything she does has grace and charm, a fascinating Oriental quality. Look at her eyes, Harry, her mouth, her young virgin voluptuousness. Oh, God, you don't know how much I love this woman, Harry. I can't bear being away from her. Not even for a minute. It's sheer torture.

HARRY. Why don't you get a divorce?

MILT. All I have to do is ask Ellen and . . . You don't know women, Harry. Say no, they'll say yes. Say yes, they'll say no. It can't be done that way. Never. Look at me, Harry. I look happy, don't I? I look as if I have everything in the world to live for. Well, I don't. I'm miserable; positively miserable.
> *Moves left, talking to photograph.*

Linda, my sweetheart, what's going to happen to us?

HARRY. (*Crosses to* MILT, *puts arm about his shoulder*) Come on, Milt; get a hold of yourself.

MILT. (*Moves right, with* HARRY's *arm still about his shoulder*) That's easy for you to say, Harry. You don't know what torture it is. We work in the same office; we can't speak to one another, we can't look at one another . . .

> *Both move left, with* HARRY *now stroking* MILT's *neck.*

We have to meet in back alleys and bus terminals and crowded, noisy saloons. Do you know what that's like? Any other woman would have given up on me long ago. But she . . . That woman . . . I tell you, I'll go out of my mind!

> *Buries his head on* HARRY's *shoulder.*

HARRY. (*Consoling him*) It couldn't be that hopeless, Milt. Why don't you . . .

MILT. (*Pulls back*) I've tried everything, everything! She won't give me a divorce. I know she won't. I wouldn't even bother asking her. I've been over this a thousand times, Harry. Linda and I do nothing else but talk about it.

> *Turns away from* HARRY *in his misery.*

There's only one answer and that's if she wants a divorce herself, if she meets someone and . . . meets someone and . . .

> *Turns to* HARRY.

> HARRY *puts his hand up in a gesture of refusal and moves to the bench and sits.*

> MILT *follows him to bench, puts arm around his shoulder and grabs his hand.*

Harry, Harry, buddy, buddy, old classmate of mine.

Pulling HARRY's *hand back and forth.*
Alma mater, alma mater, forward to the fray; we will . . .

HARRY. (*Freeing his hand and stopping* MILT) Oh, no. Definitely not. Don't ask.

MILT. Is this what I get for saving your life? Talk about gratitude! Harry, all I want you to do is meet her, just meet her.

HARRY. I said no.

MILT. (*Humbly*) Dostoyevski.

HARRY. That's not going to help. So let's drop it.

MILT. Okay. Okay. That's your privilege.
Removes jacket, folds it and places it on the bench. Runs to railing left of alcove and jumps up on it.

HARRY. (*Running after him; holds on to his knees*) Milt! Cut it out! Milt!

MILT. Let go of me!

HARRY. Don't be a fool!

MILT. How long do you think I can go on like this, living with one woman, loving another? I can't sleep, I can't eat, I can't work . . . What do you think I'm made of?

HARRY. You couldn't be serious.

MILT. Couldn't I? Look. Look at this.
He removes a large wicked-looking knife from a leather sheath on his belt. HARRY *dances away fearfully.*
Did you ask yourself why I came here tonight, Harry? Did you ask yourself what I'm doing in this godforsaken place?

HARRY. You don't mean . . .

MILT. (*Jumps down from railing*) Ellen should be here any minute. Draw your own conclusions.

> *He returns knife to sheath.*

HARRY. No. I don't believe it. That's the ugliest, the most cowardly and revolting . . . You were actually going to . . .

MILT. Yes! Yes! It's her or me. One or the other. I can't go on like this anymore, Harry. Now will you let me . . .

> *He dashes to railing.* HARRY *grabs him. They struggle.*

HARRY. No, Milt! Milt! What are you doing?

> *He throws* MILT *to ground; surprised tone.*

This isn't like you.

> *Sits on* MILT's *backside.*

You were always so levelheaded, always so damn anxious to make something of yourself and get ahead in the world. You're not going to throw it all away now, are you?

MILT. (*In despair*) I've had as much as I can take of this misery.

HARRY. Always working, from the first day of school, thinking about business, finance, investments, Wall Street . . .

MILT. (*Looking up at* HARRY) What's the good of bringing all that up? Don't you see, Harry? I've had it.

> *Clutching throat.*

Up to here, I've had it!

HARRY. But love, Milt; what about love?

MILT. Love?

HARRY. Love. The thing you were talking about only a minute ago.

> *They rise to their feet.*

MILT. Linda . . .

HARRY. Linda. Exactly.

MILT. Harry, meet her; just meet her.

HARRY. Linda?

MILT. No, no, Ellen. Meet Ellen.

HARRY. Will you promise to stop this nonsense?

MILT. I promise. Yes.

HARRY. And the . . .
> Points to knife.

MILT. No more. I promise.

HARRY. Let me have it.
> HARRY *takes the knife from him. Suddenly, un-*
> *expectedly, he turns, throws knife at sandbox; it*
> *sticks, vibrates rapidly. A mechanical device can*
> *be used so that it appears as if he has thrown the*
> *knife but in fact the knife is concealed and a*
> *second knife is sprung from sandbox.* HARRY *falls*
> *back into* MILT, *amazed by his own expertness.*

MILT. (*Staring at knife in sandbox, with admiration*) Just
meet her, Harry. I know you two will hit it off. She reads,
Harry, book after book after book. And she paints, and she
plays guitar . . .

HARRY. (*Puts jacket on* MILT, *buttons it*) Classical or flamenco?

MILT. What's that?

HARRY. The guitar. Does she play classical or flamenco?

MILT. I don't really . . .

HARRY. I play flamenco.

MILT. She's good at it; very good at it, whatever it is. And she reads, Harry. That woman reads continuously, books I never heard of . . . with hard covers, too!

HARRY. All right. I'll meet her. But that's all I'll do.

MILT. That's all I want you to do.

HARRY. Don't forget your promise.

MILT. I won't. You have my word on it.

> ELLEN's *footsteps are heard off right.*

Did you hear . . . That's her. She's coming.

> *Leads* HARRY *to alcove, left.*

Wait here, Harry. I'll bring her over. Wait right here. Don't move.

> MILT *hurries to right where he meets* ELLEN *as she enters. She wears a mink coat, skirt, blouse of same color, alligator bag and shoes, a black kerchief on her head, a pair of dark sunglasses; she carries a rolled graph, about three feet long— a window shade in a wooden casing.* HARRY *tactfully leans over the railing and stares at the river below.*

MILT. Ellen, where were you? I was getting worried.

> *He removes her kerchief and sunglasses, puts them on bench.*

You'll never guess what happened. I ran into an old friend of mine. Harry Berlin. Remember me telling you about Harry Berlin?

> *He unbuttons her coat, straightens blouse; on his knees he puts his hand under her dress and pulls her slip down.*

We roomed together at Polyarts U. I want you to meet him, El. He's a wonderful guy. You two are going to love one another.

*He takes comb from his breast pocket, starts
combing and "teasing" her hair, extravagantly
with the finicky adroitness of a couturier. He goes
on for a while before he speaks.*

I want Harry to see what a lucky guy I am. There that does
it.

*He hums contentedly; when he is done he takes
compact from her pocketbook: moves her to lamppost for better light, tilts her head back; puts lip-
stick on her mouth; blots her lips with Kleenex
and rouges her cheeks with a long rouge brush he
takes from his breast pocket.*

It was the funniest thing. I came up here to meet you and
there he was, like he is now, leaning over the rail. I recog-
nized him at once. But he's changed, El. You're going to
have to be nice to him. He's been through hell, the poor
guy. Don't you remember me telling you about him? Top
man at Polyarts U. The fellows used to call him Dostoyevski. What a guy. Plays a terrific guitar. He's sick now. Needs
encouragement. Love. A reason for living. Don't get fright-
ened if he has a fit. He comes right out of them. Poor guy.

*He holds compact under her mouth; she spits un-
inhibitedly on cake mascara;* MILT *stands behind
her, energetically rubbing brush on mascara; tilt-
ing her head forward, he applies it to her eyes.*

We have to darken these. Does wonders for your eyes.
Gives them a deep almost Oriental look. There, there,
that's better.

*Returns compact to her pocketbook, takes out
atomizer, sprays her.*

Let me see. You look positively ravishing, El; beautiful.

Returns atomizer; takes her hand.

Now come. I want . . .

ELLEN. (*Pulling free; restrained anger*) No, Milt.

MILT. Why not? He's waiting . . .

ELLEN. He can wait. I want to talk to you.
> *Returns kerchief and sunglasses to her pocket-book; places pocketbook beside bench, right.*

MILT. (*Annoyed*) El . . .

ELLEN. What I have to say will only take a few minutes. There may not be many more of them. You didn't come home until after one last night.

MILT. I told you what happened, hon. I was stuck in the office. These clients came and the boss was there and I couldn't . . .

ELLEN. (*Sharply*) Milt.

MILT. It's the truth, El!

ELLEN. It wouldn't give me any satisfaction to prove you're lying, so we'll let it stay like that. I have something to show you. I made this while you were out last night.
> *She hooks graph to lamppost.*

Let me explain it to you.
> *She pulls graph down to its full length; points with finger.*

These black vertical lines divide our five years of marriage into months; these blue vertical lines divide the months into weeks. Now. Each time this red horizontal line running across the top of the graph hits the blue vertical line, that indicates the number of sexual experiences over a seven-day period.

MILT. (*Covers graph with his body*) Ellen, for God's sake . . .
> *Looks about in embarrassment.*

We can talk about this later.

ELLEN. You're always saying later. That's a favorite play of yours. No, Milt. Not tonight. These things must be said while they still can be said.

> *Mumbling under his breath* MILT *crosses to bench, sits.*

I'd like to continue if you don't mind. Now. You'll notice on this graph how at the beginning of our marriage the red horizontal line touches the blue vertical line at a point of . . . fourteen, fifteen times a week, and how, gradually, the number of contacts become less and less until eighteen months ago, when we have an abrupt break-off, the last time being July twenty-third, the night of your sister's wedding, and after that date the red horizontal line doesn't touch the blue vertical line once, not once! I have nothing further to say, Milt.

> *She tugs down on graph so that it snaps up cleanly and disappears in the wooden casing; pause.*

When something like this is allowed to happen to a marriage, you can't go on pretending.

> *Removes graph from lamppost.*

You want to pretend. Oh, the temptation is great to overlook, to find excuses, to rationalize.

> *Waving graph.*

But here, Milt, here are the facts. Our relationship has deteriorated to such an extent that I don't feel responsible anymore for my own behavior.

MILT. (*Rises, arms held out, smiling*) Hon, you're mad at me.

ELLEN. (*Still angry*) It isn't a question of being mad at you. We've gone a long ways from that.

MILT. I see.

> *Takes graph from her.*

Just the same I'd like to ask you something, El.

ELLEN. Speak. I can't stop you.

MILT. Do you think our marriage is a failure?

ELLEN. I do.

MILT. (*Triumphantly*) I thought so. I thought that was behind it. Well, before I give you a divorce . . .

ELLEN. There isn't going to be a divorce.

MILT. There isn't?

ELLEN. We've made a mistake, but we've got to make the
best of it.

MILT. We'll act like civilized human beings.

ELLEN. I have no intention of doing otherwise.

MILT. Good.
> *Formally.*
Ellen, I'd like you to meet a friend of mine whom I acci-
dentally bumped into a little while before you came and
who is now waiting over there for us.

ELLEN. (*Stiffly*) I know what my duties are.

MILT. Then let me remind you that since he is a friend of
mine that you treat him with every courtesy and that any
kindness extended to him is considered a kindness by ex-
tension to me.

ELLEN. I understand fully.

MILT. Good. Do you have anything more to say?

ELLEN. Nothing.

MILT. Very good. So long as we understand one another.
> *Puts graph down on seat of upstage bench and
> goes to* HARRY.

Harry. Harry. Sorry to keep you waiting.

> *Arm about* HARRY, *brings him down to where* ELLEN *waits.*

Well, here she is. Harry Berlin. Ellen Manville.

> *They stare blankly at one another.*

Ellen Manville. Harry Berlin.

> *Still no reaction from them; he stands between them, arms around their shoulders.*

My two best friends.

> *Turns head quickly from one to the other; hugs them.*

My best classmate . . . My best wife . . . I've looked forward to this for years. I . . .

> *Turns head. They don't budge.*

I'll tell you what. I'm going to leave you two alone to . . . to get to know one another.

> *Slides out from between them, and begins to move left.*

I'll be back. Don't go 'way.

> *Stops, takes* HARRY *by his arm and pulls him off, left.*

Huh . . . Harry. I did a silly thing. Left the house without taking any money. Could you loan me five bucks until later?

HARRY. (*Takes out some crumpled bills and gives him one*) Is it enough?

MILT. Sure, sure, just till later . . .

> *Puts money in pocket.*

Harry, she's a wonderful girl. But she's had a terribly rough time of it. Try to understand her.

> *Moves left; loudly.*

See you both soon. You'll love one another, I know you will.

Picks up coat and exits. In a second he pops back in, grabs the basket in one jerk and exits.

There is a long uncomfortable pause. ELLEN *takes out a cigarette from a package in her coat pocket, lights it, and leans against the lamppost, front.*

HARRY *buttons his shirt, takes a ready-made tie from his jacket pocket, and hooks it onto his collar. He carefully buttons his jacket and brushes his pants. After preparing himself, he crosses to* ELLEN's *right and grabs the lamppost with one hand.*

HARRY. Classical or flamenco?

ELLEN. Flamenco.

HARRY. Me, too.
Sings a few bars of a flamenco melody. There is no response. A slight pause. HARRY *points out over audience.*
That's the Empire State Building over there.

ELLEN. (*Without looking; wrapped in her own suffering*) I know.

HARRY. I'd like to go there sometime.

ELLEN. I wouldn't.

HARRY. You wouldn't?

ELLEN. I wouldn't.

HARRY. You're probably right.
Takes off tie and puts it back into his pocket, unbuttons collar and jacket, moves back to the bench and sits left. A pause. HARRY *looks up.*
A star . . . First one. You can hardly see it, it's so weak.

"Starlight, starbright, first star I see tonight, wish I may, wish I might . . ."

>To ELLEN.

Make a wish.

ELLEN. I wish . . . I wish I was a lesbian.

HARRY. (*Slowly turns and looks at her*) You don't mean that.

ELLEN. (*Throws down cigarette and grinds it under her shoe*) I do. I certainly do. Then I wouldn't have all these demeaning problems.

>*Again leans against lamppost.*

HARRY. You'd have other problems.

ELLEN. Like what?

HARRY. Like picking up girls, for one.

ELLEN. (*Bitterly*) That would be simple. All I'd have to do is learn how to be a liar and a hypocrite.

HARRY. There's a lot more to it than that. Do you know what you have to pay for a haircut these days?

ELLEN. I'd pay for it. Gladly. Anything but this heartache; anything.

>*Puts her hand up and grabs lamppost.*

HARRY. Look, you don't have to stay if you don't want to. I can tell Milt . . .

ELLEN. I have nothing else to do.

HARRY. The same here.

>*Pause.* ELLEN *leans against the lamppost, stares up at the sky, one hand clutching the post and one foot pressed to it. She starts to sing in a deep lugubrious voice, softly at first, almost to herself, but with obvious feeling. She is indifferent to* HARRY *who shifts about on the bench nervously.*

33]

ELLEN. (*Sings*)
   Love cast its shadow over my heart.
   Love changed my life right from the start.

HARRY. (*Uncomfortably*) I know, Milt told me everything.

ELLEN. (*Sings*)
   I cried it couldn't be,
   Then Love laughed back at me.

HARRY. It'll work out all right.

ELLEN. (*Sings*)
   Why did you come?
   Why did you stay?

HARRY. You have to be patient with him.

ELLEN. (*Sings, opening her coat*)
   Why did you take me,
   Only to play?
   Oh, Love. Love. Love. Love.
   Look what you've done to me.

HARRY. (*Shrugging, with a sigh*) Well . . . Sometimes it happens that way.

ELLEN. (*Wipes a tear from her eye*) I am sorry. I'm afraid I'm not myself tonight.

HARRY. Don't apologize.

ELLEN. (*Leaves post and looks about*) It is nice out.

HARRY. Probably rain soon.

ELLEN. (*Moves downstage and looks out over audience*) How far down do you think it is?

HARRY. Far enough.

ELLEN. You know, I'm afraid of water. I can't swim a stroke.

[34

But tonight . . . with the moon shining on it, it looks quite beautiful and . . . and almost inviting.

HARRY. You shouldn't talk like that.

ELLEN. Shouldn't I? Harry, what do you think I did with my life? What do you think made me the way I am? You don't have to answer that. When I look back . . .
> *Looks out once more.*

It couldn't have worked out very differently. My childhood was impossible, absolutely impossible. My parents separated when I was three. I spent six months with one, six months with the other; they passed me back and forth like an old sack.

HARRY. That was a lot better than I did.
> *Rises; moves left.*

My folks left me with my grandparents. I saw them maybe once every four or five years. It was hell, Ellen; believe me, it was hell.

ELLEN. Not as bad as what I went through, Harry. Oh, no.

HARRY. Worse than what you went through, Ellen; lots worse.

ELLEN. You ever live with an alcoholic?

HARRY. My grandfather drank . . .

ELLEN. Enough to have delirium tremens?

HARRY. (*Wagging his hand*) He used to shake a little . . .

ELLEN. Well, it's not the same thing, oh, no, Harry, it's not the same thing.

HARRY. (*Foiled*) Anyone ever call you a bastard?

ELLEN. A relative or a stranger?

HARRY. A relative.
> *No answer.*

Well, they called me one.

ELLEN. I never had a birthday party.

HARRY. I didn't know when my birthday was until I got a notice from my draft board.

ELLEN. Did anyone ever try to rape you?

HARRY. (*Thoughtfully*) Ahh . . .

ELLEN. I said, "Did anyone ever try to rape you?" When I was fifteen, Harry, only fifteen. Two boys . . . If I hadn't kicked and screamed . . .

HARRY. Where was it?

ELLEN. Where was what?

HARRY. That the two boys grabbed you.

ELLEN. (*Holding head in hands; traumatically*) In Queens. On Parsons Boulevard. When I was walking home from the bus stop.

HARRY. (*Vehemently*) I've never been to Parsons Boulevard. Never. I don't even know where the hell Parsons Boulevard is!

> ELLEN *crosses to* HARRY.

ELLEN. I was lonely, Harry; I was always lonely.

> HARRY *moves upstage and begins to walk along rail to the right.* ELLEN *follows him, pulling at his sleeve.*

There was no one for me to talk with, or share things with. I couldn't make friends because I never stayed in one place long enough. I went deeper and deeper inside of myself. I read and fantasized and was far too bright for my age. And before I knew it I had grown up, life was for real.

> *They continue offstage and with* ELLEN *talking*

incessantly, turn and come back on, moving to
the left of the alcove.

On the one hand, I possessed a cold calculating mind; it
was sharp as a razor, incisive, penetrating. Men were afraid
of me. They were afraid of my mind, my power of analysis,
my photographic memory. They wouldn't discuss things
with me. They became resentful and standoffish and
avoided me because I was a threat to their feelings of
masculine superiority.

ELLEN *stops* HARRY *and both turn downstage.*

Ask me a question, Harry.

HARRY. How many states did Al Smith win in the election of
1928?

ELLEN. In the election of 1928 the presidential candidate
Alfred E. Smith won eight states: they were the states of
Arkansas, Alabama, Georgia, Louisiana, Massachusetts,
Mississippi, Rhode Island and South Carolina.

HARRY. (*Nodding, shakes* ELLEN'*s hand*) It's been very nice
speaking to you, Ellen. But I really have to go. Tell
Milt . . .

ELLEN. Please, Harry. Stay. Don't go yet.

Stops him, and again begins to move right along
the railing with him.

You see, on the other hand, on the other hand, Harry. I
was a woman, a woman who wanted to be loved, who
wanted to have children, who wanted all the common
dreary horrible middle-class things . . .

HARRY *turns back and wearily moves left, leaning*
on the railing. ELLEN *not noticing, continues off*
right.

things that every other woman takes for granted. I willingly . . .

ELLEN *realizes he is no longer with her, and turns and runs left after him. Catching up with him, she continues.*

I willingly succumbed to biological and sociological necessity. I willingly confessed my womanhood. But how do I bridge the gap? I didn't ask for universal education. Why was I educated, Harry, if I'm compelled to live this fractured existence?

HARRY. (*Angrily; moves to sandbox and sits*) Nobody thinks of these things until it's too damn late!

ELLEN. (*Moves right to bench, sits*) Now there's so little to believe in, so little to keep me going.

HARRY. Love?

ELLEN. Love?

HARRY. Love. What about love?

ELLEN. Oh, I don't know. Once. Yes. Once.

HARRY. Once is enough. It's more than most people had.

ELLEN. You know nothing about women, Harry. For a woman to have never known love isn't tragic. The dream is still there. The dream . . . She needs that more than she does the reality. But to have love become a shabby cynical emotion . . . To watch it change into pettiness and hate . . . That's what destroys her. She loses her dream and . . .
Through clenched teeth.
It makes an animal of her, a vicious little creature who only thinks of scratching and biting and getting revenge. Look, Harry, look!
She pulls a large unsheathed bread knife from inside her coat; rises. HARRY *looks from the knife in her hand to the one beside him sticking into the sandbox.*

Do you know what I was going to do with this?

HARRY. You don't mean . . . ?

ELLEN. (*Moves to left, stabbing air viciously*) Yes. Milt Manville! Milt Manville! I was going to use it on him.

> HARRY *gets up and moves upstage to* ELLEN's *right. She turns to him.*

I can't go on like this anymore, Harry. I know he's lying to me. I know he's seeing another woman.

> ELLEN *again turns left and slashes the air.*

I won't have it! I won't let him!

HARRY. Ellen, don't, he's not worth . . .
> *Moves toward her.*

ELLEN. (*Suddenly turning with knife so that* HARRY *has to jump back to avoid being slashed*) What's left for me? I don't make friends easily. I can't start again. Don't you see, there's only one thing . . . Only . . .
> *Grabs knife in both hands and raises it over her head.*

Yes! Yes!

> HARRY *grabs her wrists with both hands and struggles with her to prevent her from plunging the knife into her chest.*

HARRY. Give it to me. Give it . . .

ELLEN. Leave me, Harry. Please . . .

HARRY. A smart girl like you . . .

ELLEN. I want it this way. Please . . . Please . . .
> *The knife turns in her hand and is now pointed at* HARRY's *Adam's apple. He leans over backward to prevent being stabbed until he is lying supine on the ground, with* ELLEN, *in a state of hysteria,*

> *bent over him and trying, without knowing it, to*
> *plunge the knife into him.*

HARRY. No, no, Ellen . . .

ELLEN. I won't have it. I won't!

HARRY. What are you . . .

ELLEN. Good-bye, Harry!

HARRY. For cryin' out loud . . .

ELLEN. Good-bye, everyone!

HARRY. You crazy bitch, will you cut it out!

> HARRY *finally manages to turn the knife aside.*
> *The knife drops to the ground. She stands erect,*
> *steps over* HARRY, *and moves to the bench; she*
> *weeps quietly into her hands.* HARRY, *after several*
> *attempts, manages to get up. He crosses up to the*
> *rail and leans over it; retches hollowly. He then*
> *picks up the knife and moves to* ELLEN, *offering*
> *her his handkerchief.*

ELLEN. (*Taking handkerchief*) Thank you.

HARRY. (*Now offers knife*) Do you want this?
> *She shakes her head.*

Are you sure?
> *She nods and he puts knife into his jacket pocket.*
You're not going to be this dumb again, are you?

ELLEN. No, Harry. I am sorry.

HARRY. (*Buttons her coat*) You promise?

ELLEN. I promise.

HARRY. All right. Let's forget it.
> *And suddenly, unexpectedly,* HARRY *takes the*
> *knife from his pocket, whirls to the left and hurls*

the knife at the sandbox; a second knife appears downstage of the first, vibrating rapidly. HARRY *moves away with a slight swagger and sits down at the right of the bench.*

ELLEN. (*Sits next to him and returns handkerchief to him, placing her head on his shoulder*) I've been a great deal of trouble to you.

HARRY. Forget it.
>   Gets up and moves downstage, sitting on the curb.

ELLEN. (*Moves downstage and sits to the right of* HARRY) I don't often meet people who take kindness for granted.

HARRY. (*Moves away*) Forget it.

ELLEN. (*She moves to him*) I have to tell you . . .

HARRY. (*Turning, shouting*) I said forget it! Forget it!
>   Rises and moves left away from her.
What's wrong with you? You're giving me a headache!
>   Wailing.
Have a little pity for the next guy.
>   Sits down on sandbox.

ELLEN. (*Pause*) I am sorry, Harry.

HARRY. (*Without turning*) That's all right.

ELLEN. Milt has spoken about you. Frequently.

HARRY. It's fifteen years since I saw him.

ELLEN. He has nothing but good things to say.

HARRY. I changed. I changed a lot.

ELLEN. You were something of a father figure to him.

HARRY. (*Turning to her*) He never told me that.

41]

ELLEN. You know how he is.
> *Gets up and moves left.*

HARRY. He should have told me. I could have helped him with his homework.

ELLEN. Harry, isn't there anything . . .

HARRY. Nothing. For me . . . there's nothing.

ELLEN. You can't mean that.

HARRY. I can't. Ha, ha!

ELLEN. You've never been in love, have you?

HARRY. Love?

ELLEN. Love. It's there. In all of us.

HARRY. But I thought . . .

ELLEN. It's hard to kill a dream, Harry.
> *Sings romantically, directing the song to* HARRY.
Love cast its shadow over my heart,
Love changed my life right at the start,
I cried it couldn't be,
> *Moves to* HARRY *and unbuttons coat.*
Then Love laughed back at me.
Oh, why did you come?
Why did you stay?
> *Touches his face with her hand.*
Why did you take me,
> *Lifts his hand and brings it slowly, steadily upward.*
Only to play?
Oh, Love. Love. Love. Love.
Look what you've done to me.
> *Places his hand on her breast and closes the coat over it.*

HARRY. (*As she sings, shifts about agitatedly*) Ellen, stop it; that's enough . . . Why don't you sit down? I want to speak to you, tell you something about myself. I . . . You don't know me, Ellen. I'm a dead man. Dead inside. Dead to everyone and . . . everything. Ellen, will you stop that damn singing! I'm trying to explain. I'm not the kind of man you think. I can't change.

> *In despair.*

What's the good? The jig's up. The chips are down. No way out.

> *Softly.*

Ellen . . . Ellen . . .

> *As she places his hand on her breast,* HARRY *bolts upright, his eyes widen, and he begins to sing with a great fervor.*

Love cast its shadow over my heart,
Love changed my life right from the start.
Da, da, da, dum, de, dum . . .

> HARRY *gets up and taking* ELLEN *in his arms, with great style and grace and with a formal dip, begins to waltz her about the stage.*

ELLEN. (*Exultantly*) Dance with me, Harry; dance.

HARRY. It's been years . . .

ELLEN. Turn me! Turn me!

HARRY. It's fun. I'm having fun!

ELLEN. Let yourself go, Harry!

HARRY. I feel like singing at the top of my lungs!

ELLEN. Then sing, Harry, sing!

> *Holding hands and carried by the momentum of their emotions, they both sing the following lines superbly as though an aria.*

HARRY. (*Singing*) Oh, Ellen, I think I'm in love with you.

ELLEN. (*Singing*) Oh, Harry, can it possibly be?

HARRY. (*Singing*) I never felt this way before.

ELLEN. (*Singing*) My heart is beating like a banging door.

HARRY. (*Singing*) Oh, how good it feels to be in love with someone like you.

> *They kiss, sink slowly to their knees,* ELLEN *ending cradled in* HARRY's *arms.*

ELLEN. (*Looking up at him*) Dostoyevski.

HARRY. Ellen Manville.

ELLEN. (*Rises to her knees*) I didn't really think it could happen to me again.

HARRY. I feel like a kid, all weak and sticky inside. Is that . . .

ELLEN. That's part of it. Say it, Harry.

HARRY. Say what?

ELLEN. Just say it!

HARRY. You don't mean . . . ?

ELLEN. Yes, yes, say it!

HARRY. I . . . Ellen, it isn't easy. I never . . .

ELLEN. Say it! Say it!

HARRY. (*With great difficulty; voice distorted unnaturally and only after several attempts*) I la . . . I la . . . I . . . I . . . I l-o-o-o-o-ve . . . ye . . . ye . . . you.

ELLEN. Oh, Harry.

> *They kiss and then rise.*

Harry, do you still feel that there's nothing . . .

HARRY. Don't say it. No. Life . . . Life is a mystery.

ELLEN. (*Turns downstage*) Do you hear the birds singing?

HARRY. (*Behind her, with his arms around her*) Yes, yes.
      Gesturing.
Here, birdies; here, birdies . . .

ELLEN. Do you see the sun?

HARRY. It's a beautiful sun.

ELLEN. It's our sun, Harry.

HARRY. Sun, I love you!

ELLEN. It's all happening so quickly. I'm dizzy.

HARRY. Me, too. Ellen . . . You say it.

ELLEN. You want me to say it?

HARRY. Yes. Say it. Please.

ELLEN. Harry . . .
      Inhaling deeply.
Harry . . . I like you very much.

HARRY. Like me?

ELLEN. (*Turns to* HARRY) I think you're one of the nicest and most thoughtful people I ever met.

HARRY. What're you talking about?

ELLEN. Isn't that what you wanted me to say?

HARRY. (*Angrily*) No. No. Not on your life! You say what I say. I said it. Now you say it. Fair is fair!

ELLEN. (*Sits down on the bench*) But, Harry, I don't know. Really. I've been hurt once and . . . it's just that I have to be sure. I'm confused. I wasn't prepared for anything like this . . . I . . .
      Turns left to HARRY.
Harry, *how much* do you love me?

HARRY. (*Moves to the bench; outburst*) A lot! An awful lot!

ELLEN. But *how much?*

HARRY. (*Slight pause; begins to answer; gives it up*) I see what you mean.

ELLEN. It's a problem. Love isn't a commodity that you can measure. And yet there are different degrees of it. We have to know what we can expect from one another. Am I the first woman you ever loved, Harry? The truth, now.

HARRY. I swear, Ellen. That's the truth. Before I came on this bridge tonight, I never looked twice at any woman.

ELLEN. But you did sleep with other women, didn't you, Harry?

HARRY. And you? What about you?

ELLEN. (*Rises, gets graph from upstage bench, and hands it to him*) Here. Read this. It contains the whole story. But remember, he was my husband, it had nothing to do with personal likes or dislikes. How many, Harry? I'd like to know.

HARRY. Ellen, I don't remember, I couldn't . . .

ELLEN. An approximate figure will do. I just . . .

HARRY. Twenty-eight!

ELLEN. (*Slight pause*) Twenty-eight different women or one woman twenty-eight times.

HARRY. Six women once and one woman twenty-two times.

ELLEN. Who was she, Harry?

HARRY. I . . . Ellen, I . . .

ELLEN. (*Firmly*) I want to know who she was, Harry.

HARRY. (*In exasperation*) Gussie Gooler! Gussie Gooler! But it wasn't love, Ellen. We were kids. Dumb foolish stupid kids. Her brother was my best friend!

ELLEN. Thank you for being honest.

HARRY. Is Milt the only one?

ELLEN. The only one.

HARRY. (*Waves graph before setting it down to the right of the sandbox*) I'll read this tonight.

ELLEN. (*Softly*) Harry.
> *They embrace.*

HARRY. You do love me, don't you?

ELLEN. You know I do.

HARRY. How much, Ellen? Tell me.

ELLEN. That's the very problem we're faced with.

HARRY. You're right. That's the problem.
> HARRY *suddenly stamps on* ELLEN's *upstage foot; she howls, hops on the other to the right of the bench.*

ELLEN. Owwwww! What did you do that for?

HARRY. (*Grinning sheepishly*) Do you still love me?

ELLEN. (*Slight pause*) Yes . . .
> *Limps to him.*
Yes, I do.

HARRY. There, there, that proves it! If you could love me after I did something like that to you, there isn't any . . .
> ELLEN *pulls back her arm and punches* HARRY *savagely in the stomach.* HARRY *doubles over in pain, gasps for breath.*

ELLEN. (*Bending over him*) Has your love for me changed, Harry?
> HARRY *is unable to answer.*
Has it, Harry?

HARRY. No. No. It's . . . It's all right.
>*Forces himself erect.*

ELLEN. Now I know I didn't make a mistake!
>HARRY *embraces her, with his arms around her, from behind.*
And I will be a good wife to you. I have no qualms about getting a job, working, anything, until you get back on your feet. I've learned a good deal being married to Milt and this time, I know, I . . .
>HARRY, *as she talks, grabs the top of her blouse and rips the front of it down.*

HARRY. Well?

ELLEN. (*Gulping down her anger, staring at torn blouse*) I love you, Harry.

HARRY. The same as before?

ELLEN. The same.

HARRY. (*Takes her in his arms*) Harry Berlin is happy! For the first time in fifteen years Harry Berlin is actually happy!
>*In his exuberance leaves her and steps up on sand-box.*
I'm not going to disappoint you, Ellen. I'll come out of it.
>ELLEN *reaches into her coat pocket and takes out a pair of scissors. She quietly crosses to* HARRY, *as he talks, and cuts the piece of rope holding up his pants. They fall about his ankles and she puts the scissors back in her pocket.*
I'll make good. I know I will. I don't need anything but what I got. I . . .
>HARRY *stops, looks down at his pants. He closes his jacket about himself, modestly.*

ELLEN. Have your feelings for me decreased in any way, Harry?

> *Slight pause.*

Have they, Harry?

HARRY. (*Arms crossed*) It's cold.

ELLEN. I asked you a question, Harry.

HARRY. I love you, Ellen.

ELLEN. Despite everything.

HARRY. Despite everything.

ELLEN. Oh, Harry . . .

> *She gets up on sandbox and embraces him. During the embrace he reaches down, pulls up his pants and fastens them.*

HARRY. (*In curt, businesslike tone*) Ellen . . .

ELLEN. Yes, Harry.

HARRY. Do you love me, Ellen?

ELLEN. I love you.

HARRY. Please turn around.

ELLEN. Harry . . .

HARRY. Do what I told you.

ELLEN. (*Gets down from sandbox*) I love you, Harry.

HARRY. I love you. Now do what I told you.

> ELLEN *turns around.* HARRY *quickly rips the mink coat off her and in a single gesture hurls it over the railing.*

ELLEN. (*Running to railing*) My coat! My coat!

> *After looking over railing she turns and doubles*

> *over in a fit of soundless hysteria.* HARRY *takes her in his arms and leads her, writhing and floundering about, to the bench. He finally gets her to sit down.*

HARRY. Do you still love me?

ELLEN. (*Shouting*) I bought it with my own money!

HARRY. Yes or no? Do you love me or don't you?

ELLEN. (*Sobbing*) I love you.

HARRY. (*Embraces her*) I love you, too, Ellen. I can't believe it.
> *Rises.*

Everything's clearing up for me. I have the feeling I can start writing poetry again. I wrote tons of it at school.
> *Reciting.*

"Under the starlit window, two lovers lie in bed; naked up to their shoulders, for neither has a head. One lover touches the other, the other . . ."

ELLEN. (*Coolly; rising*) Harry.

HARRY. (*Going to her*) Yes, Ellen . . . Darling.

ELLEN. May I have your jacket?

HARRY. My jacket?

ELLEN. Please give it to me.

HARRY. Ellen . . .

ELLEN. I said, please give it to me.
> *He gives her his jacket.*

Harry, I love you.

HARRY. I love you, Ellen.

ELLEN. I know you do.

> *Slight pause.*

Harry . . .

> ELLEN *gestures upstage.* HARRY *follows her glance to river.*

Good-bye.

HARRY. You don't mean . . . ?

ELLEN. (*Turning downstage; emotionally, burying her face in his coat*) I can't watch! I can't!

HARRY. (*Nodding; resignedly*) Good-bye, Ellen.
> *Moves to railing.*

ELLEN. (*Sobbing into hands*) Good-bye, my dearest; good-bye.

HARRY. (*Moves downstage*) I . . . I love you.

ELLEN. I love you! I love you!

> HARRY *climbs up on the railing right of the alcove; he is about to throw himself into the river when* MILT *comes in down left.* MILT, *seeing* HARRY, *drops the overcoat he is carrying which is now of enormous size, and running to rail grabs* HARRY *about the legs. He attempts to pull him down but* HARRY *holds on tightly to the cable.*

MILT. Harry! Harry! For God's sake!

HARRY. Get away . . .

MILT. Listen to me.
> *Trying to pull him down.*

HARRY. Let go!
> *Kicking at* MILT.

MILT. Love, Harry, love!

HARRY. That's what it is, you damn ass! Now will you let . . .

ELLEN. (*After putting on* HARRY's *jacket runs to him*) No, Harry. Don't. You don't have to. It's true. It's really, really true!

HARRY. Ellen!

> HARRY *slides down the cable to the ground, and embraces* ELLEN. *They kiss.* MILT *stands nearby, viewing them critically.*

MILT. (*Slight pause*) What's going on here?

ELLEN. (*Breaking the embrace*) You tell him.

HARRY. No, you better tell him.

ELLEN. I think it wiser if you told him.

HARRY. Do you think so?

ELLEN. I do, Harry.

HARRY. Okay.

> *Kisses her hand, crosses to* MILT.

Milt, it worked out all right. We're in love and we'd like . . .

> *Turns to* ELLEN.

We'd like to get married.

> ELLEN *comes to* HARRY *and they embrace.* MILT *quietly watches.*

MILT. I see. Leave my best friend with my wife alone and this is what happens. You ought to be ashamed of yourself. The both of you!

> MILT *moves down left.* ELLEN *follows down after him and* HARRY *comes to her right and puts his arms about her.*

ELLEN. Milt, I want a divorce. And the sooner you give it to me the easier it'll be for all of us.

MILT. A divorce. I see. Five years of marriage and you come up to me and say, "Milt, I want a divorce," and I'm supposed to take it all, say nothing and go right along with this preposterous and morally contemptible idea!

HARRY. Come on, Milt. Cut it out. You know . . .

MILT. (*Sharply*) Never mind what I know, Harry. This is between my wife and myself. It has nothing to do with you. Not yet, at any rate.

ELLEN. Milt, we haven't been happy together. It's obvious that our marriage has failed.

MILT. Not completely, El. We've had some good times. Hon, remember when we first moved into our place and the painter locked himself in the bathroom and couldn't get out?

> *He breaks into uncontrollable laughter, which she joins.*

ELLEN. He was banging and screaming . . .

MILT. And the people next door . . .

> *Takes* ELLEN *in his arms and moves her away from* HARRY, *to his left.*

ELLEN. The people next . . .

MILT. They thought . . .

ELLEN. They thought . . .

MILT. He was your father . . .

> HARRY *attempts to separate* MILT *and* ELLEN.

ELLEN. That he came to take me back and you two were . . .

MILT. We two . . .

ELLEN. Were fighting . . .

> HARRY, *having failed to separate or get between*

53]

> *them, grabs the bottom of* ELLEN's *jacket and*
> *tries to pull her back.*

MILT. (*Rubbing tears from his eyes*) What a time.

HARRY. Ellen.

ELLEN. (*Ignoring him*) That was really something.

HARRY. (*Louder*) Ellen!

MILT. (*Suddenly grim; holding* ELLEN *from* HARRY) She's still my wife, Harry, and so long as she's my wife I have the right to talk to her without your interrupting!

ELLEN. (*Conciliatory, takes* MILT *right to bench*) Milt, we have to reach a decision.

MILT. I only want what's best for you, hon.
> ELLEN *sits on bench.*

HARRY. Does she get a divorce or doesn't she?

MILT. (*Turns back to* HARRY) Do you think you know this woman well enough so that you can talk of marriage? What do you know about her? You met her twenty minutes ago, Harry; only twenty minutes ago. Do you know that her mother was an alcoholic? That she can't see without glasses? that she shaves her legs and never cleans the razor?

ELLEN. (*Protestingly*) Milt . . .

HARRY. I love her, Milt.

MILT. Love. That's a fancy word. Well, before I give my consent to this marriage, Harry, I'm going to make sure that you kids know what you're doing. I'm not having this woman go through the same lousy deal she had with me, twice! Oh, no. I'm not going to let it happen.
> *Turning to* ELLEN; *quietly.*
Hon, do you know that he's a sick man, that he has fits?

ELLEN. I know, Milt . . .

MILT. Are you sure . . .

ELLEN. I love him.

MILT. He doesn't have a job.

HARRY. I'm getting a job.

MILT. (*To* HARRY, *snapping*) What kind of job?

ELLEN. (*Pleadingly*) Milt.

MILT. (*To* ELLEN) All right. All right. If that's what you want . . .

> *Moves down left with his back to bench.*

I'll give you a divorce, hon.

> HARRY *crosses to bench, sits and embraces* ELLEN.

But don't depend on me for anything. You're both old enough to know your own minds.

> *Moves up right and kneels on upstage bench between them.*

Don't come to me asking for help, money, alimony, legal fees, or anything like that because you won't get it. You make it on your own or you don't make it.

> *Behind them, hands on their shoulders; as a blessing.*

Love one another, live moderately, work together toward a common goal, show patience and consideration for each other's needs and desires, respect each other as individuals during the good times and the bad, and you'll make a go of it. El . . .

> *He kisses her on cheek.*

Every happiness. Harry . . .

> *Shaking his hand.*

You're getting a wonderful girl. Nobody knows that better than I do. Take care of her.

55]

> MILT *moves left,* HARRY *follows him.*

HARRY. Thanks. Ahhh . . .
> *Holding* MILT's *arm; whispering.*
Say, Milt, that five bucks . . .
> ELLEN *takes comb out of bag and fixes hair.*

MILT. She's a wonderful girl, Harry. You're a lucky guy.

HARRY. I know. But that five . . .

MILT. You speaking to me, Harry?

HARRY. Who do you think I'm speaking to?

MILT. That's funny. I can't hear a word you're saying.
> *Cheerfully.*
Something's wrong. Speak slowly, Harry, I'll try to read your lips.
> ELLEN *comes up to them.*

HARRY. (*Drawing out words*) That five bucks you took from me, I . . .
> *He glances down to see* ELLEN *staring up at him.*

ELLEN. What is it, Harry?

HARRY. (*Not wanting her to know*) I . . . I just . . .

ELLEN. You can tell me. I want to help you. That's why I'm here. Only to help you and be with you.

HARRY. (*Softly*) Ellen . . .

ELLEN. My Harry . . .

HARRY. Empire State Building?

ELLEN. Yes. Yes. The Empire State Building.
> *Hand in hand, they run off right, laughing happily.*

MILT. (*Watches them go, then cries out in ecstasy*) Linda! Oh, my Linda!

He runs right, jumps on the bench and springs to the crossbar of the lamppost, around which he revolves, singing joyfully, his knees curled under him.

Love cast its shadow over my heart, etc.

CURTAIN

END OF ACT I

ACT TWO

THE TIME:
Several months later: early evening.

THE SCENE:
The same as Act I.

ELLEN *is seated on the right of the downstage bench, in a black leather coat, black high-neck sweater and skirt. She is wearing black tights and low-cut black boots, with a large copper necklace and large hanging copper earrings. Her hair is now in a ponytail, and she is reading a paperback copy of* The Second Sex.

Riding a small Valmobile motor scooter, staring straight ahead, MILT *crosses the bridge, right to left above the bench, and exits. He immediately re-enters and crosses to above the bench, where he stops. He is now wearing a bright brown and yellow flecked sports jacket with a yellow shirt and olive tie, brown slacks, and brown shoes. A brown visored cap completes his outfit. Both he and* ELLEN *speak with exaggerated cheerfulness.*

MILT. (*As he stops the scooter*) El? Ellen? Is that you?

ELLEN. (*As if trying to recall who he is*) Milt. Milt Manville.

MILT. This is incredible.

ELLEN. Isn't it? You're the last . ▪ ▪

[58

MILT. How are you, El?
>*Gets off scooter.*

ELLEN. Fine. Fine. You?

MILT. (*Parks scooter and shuts off motor*) Fine. Fine.

ELLEN. Linda?

MILT. Couldn't be better.
>*Puts cap aside.*

Harry?

ELLEN. (*With inarticulate admiration*) Ahhh, he's . . .

MILT. Happy, huh?

ELLEN. Very very happy, Milt. At times it's frightening. Do I merely thank you or . . . or what?

MILT. (*Sits down left* ELLEN) I knew you were right for each other. Didn't I tell you?

ELLEN. It's more than that. Much more. It's . . .
>*Glances at wristwatch.*

In an hour or so we're going to the museum.

MILT. Is it open at night?

ELLEN. Open . . . ?
>*Breaks out in deprecating laughter.*

Oh, Milt, Milt. Milt Manville. I am sorry. So many memories come back. Yes, Milt. The Modern Museum is open every Thursday evening.

>MILT *"ahhh's," "ohhh's" and "ahummmm's, ahummmm's" all through* ELLEN's *lines, to mitigate if not destroy the sting of her remarks. When* MILT *speaks,* ELLEN *does likewise, laughing artificially, murmuring and by her approval making his remarks innocuous.*

59]

Harry and I go to museums together and we borrow books from the public library and we play flamenco duets and it's an entirely different life than what we had. Different, richer, more rewarding . . . I . . . I don't want to hurt your feelings, Milt. Let's . . .

MILT. No, no. No, you're not. I'm glad, El. It's worked out perfectly. For both of us. Linda . . .
       Smiles.
My Linda . . .
       He laughs aloud at thought her name evokes.
That woman . . . She . . . She has this dance she does before we go to bed. It's . . .
       Laughs. ELLEN *murmurs and nods agreeably.*
Some sort of Arabian belly dance. She puts a lampshade on her head, you know, and . . . She's fantastic. I don't know where she learned it but . . .

ELLEN. That's why I have the greatest and deepest respect for Harry Berlin. I learn from him. Constantly.

MILT. The same with Linda. Every day it's something else.

ELLEN. The experiences he's had, just being with him is a lesson in itself.

MILT. If I told you the things I learned from Linda . . .

ELLEN. Do you find you laugh more, Milt?

MILT. You hit it, El. That's it. That's the big difference.
       Laughing.
We get up in the morning and we start in laughing . . .

ELLEN. (*Laughing*) With Harry, too . . .

MILT. (*Laughing*) She carries on . . .

ELLEN. (*Laughing*) The tricks and jokes, he's . . .

MILT. (*Laughing*) I say, "Linda, Linda, I can't laugh more, no, I'll bust, I'll . . .
> *Suddenly overcome by misery.*

Oh, God, oh, God!

ELLEN. What is it, Milt?

MILT. I can't lie to you. Not to you, El.

ELLEN. Lie to me? About what?

MILT. She left me. Walked out.

ELLEN. When was that?

MILT. Two, three days ago. I heard from her lawyer this morning. El, I don't want to be a two-time loser. What's wrong with me? What do people have against me? Tell me. It's driving me out of my mind.

ELLEN. Perhaps you ought to go see her, speak to her, see if you can't get her to reconsider.

MILT. See who?

ELLEN. See Linda.

MILT. (*Rises and paces left*) That lazy bitch! Who wants her? She can rot in hell for all I care!

ELLEN. That's not nice, Milt.

MILT. (*Pacing*) I know it's not nice. I had to live with her!

ELLEN. You're exaggerating. She couldn't be that bad.

MILT. That's what you say.

ELLEN. You always complained that there were no surprises in our marriage. Didn't she have any surprises for you?

MILT. She had surprises. Boy, did she have surprises! As soon as we were married . . . It wasn't the same person. She was different. Physically. All over.
> *Shudders.*

She even started growing a mustache. No kidding. I mean it. I couldn't recognize her. I used to come home and think I was in the wrong apartment.

ELLEN. It's not an uncommon affliction among certain women. You should have given her sympathy, not criticism.

MILT. I should have given her shaving cream, that's what I should have given her.

ELLEN. I won't listen to you, Milt. You're being cruel and unkind. She must have had some assets for you to marry her.

MILT. (*Moves to bench, sits left of* ELLEN) El, I don't make accusations lightly, you know that, you know it's not like me; but I'm willing to bet you anything that that woman had me under the influence of drugs or . . .
Leaning toward her; ominously.
narcotics.

ELLEN. How could she have done that?

MILT. By intravenous injections. While I was sleeping.
Rolls up sleeve, shows his forearm; solemnly.
Look at this.

ELLEN. (*Examines arm*) Milt, you've had those freckles ever since I've known you.

MILT. (*Shrilly*) Purple ones? Did I ever have purple freckles?
Gets up, paces left.
I know I'm right, El. A human being couldn't change as much as she did. Overnight. Even her voice, it started coming out through her nose.
Holds fingers to nose, mimicking.
"Hey, whatta you mean by comin' in here an' leavin' the door open." That's how she sounded. It was incredible.

ELLEN. Did she at least keep the apartment clean?

MILT. Keep it clean?
> *Crosses down right, to the front of the bench.*
> *Turns back to* ELLEN.

El, hit me there.
> *Points to back.*

Go ahead. Hit me.
> *She hits him on back. A thick cloud of dust rises*
> *from his jacket.* ELLEN *coughs, waves dust away.*
> MILT *points out the floating dust.*

Now am I exaggerating? Now am I making it all up?

ELLEN. (*Contemptuously*) That's despicable. That is despicable.

MILT. She quit her job, didn't do a damn thing but lay in bed and eat bonbons all day.

ELLEN. That is ab-so-lutely despicable.
> *Heatedly.*

I'm sorry. There's just no excuse for it. None. What an obnoxious horrible foul-mouthed rat-faced lascivious woman she must have been.

MILT. She was, she . . .

ELLEN. How could you have lived with her four months? Didn't you have any pride, any sense of self-respect?

MILT. I wanted . . .

ELLEN. Would I let you leave the house in a jacket like that?

MILT. (*Shaking head*) No. No.

ELLEN. Did I lie in bed and eat bonbons all day?

MILT. (*Shaking head*) No. No.

ELLEN. Why didn't I?

MILT. Because you were good. Because you were unselfish.

ELLEN. Because I was a jerk, that's why.
> *Wipes hand on Kleenex from coat pocket.*

Because I didn't use sex instead of washing the dishes.

MILT. She did, El, she . . .

ELLEN. You don't have to draw pictures for me. Rat-faced paranoic women. All of them. I'll become ill if I continue to talk about it. You should be happy to be rid of her.

MILT. (*Pained expression*) Happy? How can I be happy?

ELLEN. Milt, there isn't someone . . . ?
> MILT *nods, lips in a pout, with the forlornness of an old man.*

You are irresponsible. There's no other word for it.
> *Impatiently; puts book in pocketbook.*

I have to go. I have my own problems, Milt. I can't spend all night . . .

MILT. I couldn't help it, El. Honest. I couldn't. Do you think I want to throw away my life like a lovesick schoolboy? But she . . . This woman here . . .
> *Takes out wallet-photograph and looks at picture so as to arouse* ELLEN's *curiosity.*

Beautiful. Too, too beautiful.
> *Moves left to center; to photograph.*

Sweetheart, if only I had the courage to speak to you . . .

ELLEN. (*Crossing to him, peering over his shoulder*) Perhaps you can arrange to . . . Let me see that.
> *Surprised.*

Milt, this is my photograph!

MILT. Of course it's your photograph.

ELLEN. You took it at your sister's wedding, the same night . . .

MILT. July twenty-third. Don't you think I know it?

ELLEN. You don't mean . . . ?

MILT. Yes! Yes!

> MILT *crosses right to bench, sits.* ELLEN *moves left.*

Oh, El . . . How stupid, how inexcusably stupid I was. I didn't realize . . . I didn't think . . . You were all I wanted. Ever, ever wanted. That first night with Linda it came to me, you, you, you, and since then I've been in such misery.

ELLEN. (*Her back to* MILT) I don't want to hear any more, Milt.

MILT. You have to, El. I've been living with this inside of me for months. It's been tearing me apart. I'm not here by accident. Harry phoned. He asked me to meet him, to collect some money I owe him. But that's not why I'm here. I came because I had to find out how you were doing, what you were doing, what chance I had . . .

ELLEN. Whatever you thought, Milt, is totally irrelevant. I'm Mrs. Harry Berlin now, and if you've made a mistake you have no one to blame but yourself.

MILT. That doesn't make it easier, El. It was my fault. Okay. I admit it. I was a stupid, selfish, hypocritical, egotistical, narrow-minded nitwit. Just like you always said. But, oh, El, hon . . .

ELLEN. (*Moves left*) No. Let's stop it now. There's nothing I can do, Milt. It's too late. Besides other considerations, Harry needs me. He depends on me.

> *Paces right to center.*

In fact If I don't get home to feed him soon he won't have any dinner.

MILT. You feed him?

ELLEN. Two-thirds water and one-third milk. That's all he'll take. He . . . He's gotten worse, Milt. He's had a great many fits and . . . It hasn't been easy for me, either. But I know what my duties are. Marriage is more than the two people involved in it. That's something you would never acknowledge. Above everything else, despite my educational background, despite my academic achievements, I want to be a good wife and a good mother. But where is the man to whom I can be a good wife? Where are the children who cry for my arms and the milk in my breasts?

MILT. (*Rises, arms outspread*) Here! Here I am!

ELLEN. You?

MILT. Yes, me.
>*Moves to* ELLEN.
Don't you see, El? I love you. I always loved you.
>ELLEN *moves away left.*
For God's sake, have pity. Don't close the door on me.

ELLEN. No, Milt. I may have the intelligence of a man . . .

MILT. Hey, listen, what was Sugar Ray Robinson's record from 1940 to 1944?

ELLEN. From 1940 to 1944 Sugar Ray Robinson had a record of fifty professional bouts. He won forty-nine, thirty-four by knockouts, fifteen by decision, and he lost only one in 1943 to a certain Jake LaMotta.

MILT. (*To himself*) I knew that schmuck last night was wrong.
>*Moves to* ELLEN.
Oh, sweetheart, I missed you so much . . .

ELLEN. (*Moving away from him*) The intelligence of a man, Milt, yes, but the emotions of a woman, the innate in-

[66

security of a woman. I refuse to be passed back and forth like an old sack.

MILT. I'd never do that.

ELLEN. You did it once.

MILT. If you gave me another chance . . .

ELLEN. You keep forgetting I'm a married woman, Milt.

MILT. (*Quacking words like a duck*) Ellie?

ELLEN. That's not going to help.

MILT. (*Still quacking*) Won't you please reconsider?

ELLEN. (*Moves down left to sandbox*) I'm in no mood for any of your games, Milt.

MILT. Okay. Okay. Listen. Just tell me you love Harry Berlin, that you're happy with him, and I'll walk away from here and, I promise, you'll never see me again.

ELLEN. Love Harry Berlin?

MILT. Just say those words and it's good-bye to Milt Manville and his silly stupid but sometimes lovable ways.

ELLEN. I . . . I can't. It's impossible. You talk about misery! Ha!

> MILT *crosses down to* ELLEN.

That makes me laugh. Misery!

> MILT *holds his hands out to her.*

You can't imagine how it's been.

> *She takes his hands and both sit down on the sandbox.*

He . . .

> *Puzzled expression.*

Who is he? What is he? Why didn't you shake me by the shoulders and slap my face and . . . do anything to stop

me? He . . . He isn't human, Milt. That man . . . He
lays in the corner of the living room, rocking on his back,
wearing a paper bag on his head, yes, a paper bag, mumbling
and groaning hour after hour . . . I have to feed him,
wash him . . . I can't tell you everything. I'm too
ashamed.

MILT. The filthy beast!

ELLEN. That's what my marriage to Harry Berlin has been
like.

MILT. Then why? Tell me why?

ELLEN. Ask me what I believe in, Milt.

MILT. What do you believe in, Ellen?

ELLEN. I believe in marriage, Milt.
        Rises, moves left.
I believe in a man coming home at five o'clock with a newspaper rolled under his arm and a silly grin on his face and
shouting, "What's for dinner, hon?" I believe in the smell
of talcum powder and dirty diapers and getting up in the
middle of the night to warm the baby's bottle. I can't
help it. I'm made that way.
        Paces up and down stage.
But why did they teach me trigonometry and biochemistry
and paleontology? Why did they so sharpen my intellect
that I find it impossible to live with a man?
        To MILT.
I'll never forgive the Board of Education for that. Never.
        Crosses up right to center.

MILT. (*Moves up to* ELLEN's *left*) If you'd listen to me . . .

ELLEN. I wouldn't have divorced you, Milt. You know that.
But you brought it about, coldly and deliberately. You

[68

forced me to marry Harry. And now I don't trust you. And where there's no trust there can't be love.

MILT. Then . . .

ELLEN. It's over.

MILT. Nothing I do or say . . .

ELLEN. (*Moves to left of bench*) The door is closed, Milt.
> MILT *nods sadly. He sings in a heartbroken voice.*

MILT. (*Sings*)
Love cast its shadow over my heart.

ELLEN. (*Sits down on bench*) Don't, Milt; please, don't.

MILT. (*Sings as he crosses to* ELLEN, *left of bench and touches her hair*)
Love changed my life right from the start.
I cried it couldn't be.

ELLEN. (*Shuddering from his touch*) We can't start all over again.

MILT. (*Turns away in anguish*)
Then love laughed back at me.
Oh, why did you come?

ELLEN. It's too late, Milt. No.
> *Flings herself on seat of bench and puts legs up over back of bench.*

MILT. (*Sings*)
Why did you stay?
Why did you take me . . .
> *Turns, sees* ELLEN, *stops in surprise. Rushing to bench, he sits and takes her in his arms.*
El . . .

ELLEN. Milt . . .
> *As she throws her arms about him, another cloud of dust rises from his jacket.*

MILT. Oh, my sweetheart.
> *They kiss.*

ELLEN. (*Staring up at him*) Dostoyevski.

MILT. No, honey. Milt. Milt Manville.

ELLEN. (*Sits up in* MILT'*s arms, with legs along bench*) Milt. Yes. Milt. Oh, I always loved you, Milt.
> *Kisses him.*

I come here almost every night, hoping you'll show up. I didn't want to marry Harry.

MILT. (*Kisses her*) You didn't want to marry Harry, did you?

ELLEN. (*Returning kisses*) You know I didn't want to marry Harry.

MILT. I know. I know.

ELLEN. I was praying you wouldn't believe what I said before.

MILT. I didn't. Honest.

ELLEN. Harry wasn't taking me to the museum tonight; he doesn't take me anyplace, not even to the movies.

MILT. I know. Now don't worry. It's all going to work out; you'll see. First thing I'm going to do, hon . . . I'm giving up my secondhand bric-a-brac and personal accessories job. I'm through working nights. I'm through scrounging in garbage pails.

ELLEN. But it means so much to you.

MILT. You mean more, much more. Our happiness means more. We're going to have to make some sacrifices, learn to do with less, budget ourselves . . . It won't be easy.
> *Rises and crosses left to trash basket.*

But every day at five I'm opening that front door and . . .
> *Picks newspaper out of trash basket.*

With this newspaper under my arm and a silly grin on my
face . . .
>*Pantomimes kicking door open.*
"What's for dinner, hon?"

ELLEN. Steak, French fries, catsup and mashed baby lima
beans, everything you like!
>*Runs to him and throws herself into his arms.*

MILT. (*Twirls her about and then puts her down*) Just the
way I like it.

ELLEN. And I'm not contradicting you anymore, Milt. Never.
Never.

MILT. One job's enough. I'm going to spend every single
evening home with you.
>*About to throw newspaper into basket, looks at it,
>has second thoughts and slips it into his side
>pocket.*

ELLEN. I'm not keeping any records and . . .
>*Steps up on sandbox.*
Ask me a question.

MILT. What countries formed the League of Nations in 1919?

ELLEN. I don't know.

MILT. You don't know?

ELLEN. (*Steps down from sandbox*) I don't know and I don't
care to know. I'm submerging my intelligence so that we
can be happy together.
>*Embraces* MILT.
That's all I want, Milt.

MILT. And all I want is you, sweetheart, and the opportunity
to be incredibly rich someday.

ELLEN. You will be; you will. But . . . Harry Berlin. What about Harry Berlin?

MILT. You'll get a divorce.

ELLEN. He'll never give it to me, Milt.

MILT. We'll have him sent away.

ELLEN. It would take years, money . . .

MILT. I thought of that. El, listen. Harry should be here any minute.
> *Looking about.*
El, he's a man who's contemplated suicide.
> *Looking about.*
If he should happen to lose his balance . . .

ELLEN. What are you saying, Milt?

MILT. If he fell off the bridge and . . .

ELLEN. No, no, don't say any more.

MILT. But it's the only way.

ELLEN. I won't have it. No.

MILT. (*Petulantly, moves up right to right of alcove at the rail*) Then you really don't love me.

ELLEN. (*Crosses up to the left of* MILT) I do, Milt.

MILT. No, you don't.

ELLEN. I do. I swear I do.

MILT. If you really loved me nothing would stand in our way. Nothing in the world!

ELLEN. Don't you understand, Milt? That's murder.

MILT. Murder? Who said anything about murder? Are you out of your mind? All I said . . .

ELLEN. We'll get into trouble. I know we will. What if we get caught?

MILT. (*Moves down right to front of bench*) You don't love me. I don't think you ever sincerely and truly loved me.

ELLEN. (*Moves down to* MILT's *left*) That isn't so.
Puts out her hand to him.

MILT. (*Pulls away from her*) Don't touch me.

ELLEN. Milt.
Moves toward him.

MILT. I said don't touch me.

ELLEN. You're being childish.

MILT. Why? Because I'm asking you to show me your love, to do this one lousy thing for me!

ELLEN. What do you want me to do?

MILT. You know.

ELLEN. Harry Berlin?
The sound of halting footsteps are heard off right.

MILT. Harry Berlin.

ELLEN. It's just that I don't think that's the answer. Can't you . . .
Hears the footsteps.
Is that him coming?

MILT. (*Looks right*) It's him. That's him.
ELLEN *begins to move left.*
Come here!
Excitedly as she comes to him.
Look, El, leave this to me. I'll take care of it.
Begins to lead her off left.

You walk down here a little. I want to speak to Harry privately. Don't listen and don't watch.

ELLEN. (*Stops and begins to protest*) You're not . . . Milt, you wouldn't . . .

MILT. (*Pushes her off left*) Just stand over . . . look. Come here.

> *They exit left.* HARRY *enters, right. He is wearing the worn velvet-collared herringbone coat which had been in the basket in the first act: unshaven, disheveled. He uses a cane, his right leg is stiff, paralyzed. He moves along, dragging his right leg, leaning on cane. He crosses between lamppost and bench and moves up left above the bench.*

HARRY. Milt . . .

> *Notices the scooter.*

Milt? Are you here, Milt? You cheap bastard, where's my five bucks?

> *Moves left to center.*

Ohhh . . . Ohhh . . . that dog. That crazy dog. On my leg. He did it on my leg. I can still feel it, wet and smelly . . . It's still there . . . Away, get away from me. Away . . .

> *Reversing the cane in his hand, he swings it at imaginary dog by his right leg. Finally turns, and with cane reversed moves up into alcove. As he does,* MILT *slowly sneaks out from down left and moves toward him, sinisterly.*

Ohhh, Ellen, my sweet, sweet, sweet Ellen. Where are you?

> HARRY *turns downstage, barely missing seeing*

MILT *who scurries back off.* HARRY *turns back to the alcove railing right.*

Ohhh, my Ellen, my sweet, sweet Ellen.

As he leans on the wrong end of the cane, it slips from beneath him and he falls to the ground. As he puts the cane down, MILT *rushes toward him to push him over the railing. When* HARRY *falls,* MILT *is unable to stop himself and dives over the right railing of the alcove.*

There is the sound of a large splash, followed by a heavy spray of water which rises above the railing and lands on HARRY. HARRY *holds out his hand to check if it's raining, looks up at the sky. Hooking one of the cables with his cane, he pulls himself erect.* ELLEN *enters left.*

ELLEN. Milt?

HARRY. (*Turning*) Ellen!

ELLEN. It's you. Where's Milt?

HARRY. Milt?

ELLEN. I thought I heard . . .

Moves right, leans over railing; softly.

Milt? Milt? I can't see a thing down there.

HARRY. (*Looking over railing in alcove*) Is he down there?

ELLEN. I don't know where he is. He was with me a minute ago. He asked . . .

Looks at HARRY.

Are you sure he wasn't here?

HARRY. I was supposed to meet him. What are you . . .

ELLEN. Never mind me. Where did he go now?

Moves to right of bench.

HARRY. He owes me five bucks. You can't trust anybody.

ELLEN. You are interested in money, aren't you, Harry?

HARRY. (*Moves downstage*) Not for myself. I wanted to buy
you something for your birthday.

ELLEN. That's very thoughtful of you. But my birthday isn't
until next August.
>   *Sits down right of bench.*

HARRY. I was saving for it. Don't start, Ellen. For cryin' out
loud. I'm a sick man. Sick! My leg.
>   *Paces left, his limp very pronounced.*

It's paralyzed. I can't move it.

ELLEN. (*Irritably*) There isn't anything wrong with your leg.

HARRY. (*Limps right*) There isn't? Then why doesn't it . . .
>   *Stops, tries to bend his right leg; to his surprise
>   it bends easily and he can raise it.*

You're right!
>   *Joyfully he flexes leg up and down; begins to run
>   in circles about the stage, tossing his cane over
>   the railing.*

It's . . . moving! It moved! I can walk again! Look, look,
I'm walking. I'm walking!

ELLEN. Harry . . . Harry, I have to speak to you. Please sit
down.
>   *Gestures to bench.*

HARRY. (*Crosses to bench, lies supine on it, his head in
ELLEN's lap*) What would I do without you? How would I
live? My own sweet precious . . . Oh, Ellen, hold me,
hold me, I need you so much . . .

ELLEN. (*Resisting*) No, Harry. Not tonight. Sit up now.
>   HARRY *gets up and sits in her lap, facing left.*

Sit up properly.

HARRY. (*Tries to embrace her*) What is it my dear one, my darling, my . . .

ELLEN. Harry, stop it and pay attention. This is important. I've tried . . . I've tried to be a good wife to you. But despite all my efforts our marriage is a failure.

HARRY. (*Dumbfounded, stops his attempts to embrace her*) Our marriage . . . a failure?

ELLEN. Yes, Harry; a failure.

HARRY. (*Crosses his right leg over his left; there is a pause*) I . . . I don't know what to say, Ellen. This is a complete shock to me. Up until this minute I thought we were a happily married couple!

ELLEN. You thought . . .

HARRY. I had no idea.

ELLEN. How could you have thought that? Didn't you hear me walking the floors nights; didn't you hear me crying in the bathroom?

HARRY. (*Shaking head*) No. No.

ELLEN. What did you think I was doing in the bathroom all night?

HARRY. (*Slight pause; desperately*) Ellen, I love you!

ELLEN. I asked you a question, Harry.
> *Bodily picks up* HARRY, *and sets him on the bench to her left.*
What do you think I was doing in the bathroom all night?

HARRY. (*Shaking his head dumbly*) I didn't want to think about it. I used to get up in the middle of the night and look at the ceiling and wonder to myself: "What could she be doing in the bathroom so long?" But I didn't want to change you, Ellen. I wanted you to be just the way you are. Is that a crime?

ELLEN. You should have made it your business to know what I was doing.

HARRY. I will. From now on . . .

ELLEN. Our marriage has been a failure from the first day. I don't have one memory worth keeping.

HARRY. Oh, no. No, Ellen. We had lots of good times. Remember . . .

ELLEN. Remember what?

HARRY. (*Slight pause; angrily*) Where's my paper hat?

ELLEN. I don't have your paper hat and you know it. Our marriage was a mistake, Harry, and anything we can do to terminate it would be a step in the right direction.

HARRY. (*Legs over* ELLEN's *lap*) I couldn't, Ellen. I'm responsible for you.

ELLEN. (*Pushes them off*) Responsible for me? You must be joking. You haven't worked a day or given me a penny since we were married.

HARRY. I was hoping to surprise you.

ELLEN. You succeeded in that.

HARRY. (*Rises; stands left of bench*) I haven't been wasting my time. I've been doing a lot of thinking, planning . . . I'm going to go back and do what I always wanted. What I should have stuck to. Go back and start right at the beginning. Ellen, in the fall I'm applying for medical school.

ELLEN. Harry, it won't do.

HARRY. All right. All right. I understand. Night calls, oper-

ations, blood all over my clothes . . . It's not all easy going. All right. Law school. In the fall I'm registering for the Bar.

ELLEN. No, Harry.

HARRY. (*Shouting in frustration*) Why not?

ELLEN. Harry, I don't love you anymore. That's all there is to it.

> *Rises and moves downstage.*

HARRY. You don't . . .

ELLEN. I doubt if I ever loved you.

HARRY. (*Moves to her, arms outstretched, fingers reaching*) Ellen, you don't know what you're saying. Love! Love!

ELLEN. What about love, Harry?

HARRY. It's . . .
> *Stops in confusion.*

ELLEN. What is it? I'd like very much to hear your definition.

HARRY. (*Raises his arms to the sky, fingers reaching*) The birds, the sun, our sun . . .

ELLEN. I don't see any sun, do you?

HARRY. Where's my paper hat?

ELLEN. I don't have your paper hat.

HARRY. (*Angrily*) Well, somebody's got my paper hat. It's not on my head, is it?

ELLEN. (*Crosses left in front of him, moves left*) You pretend love means so much to you but it doesn't, Harry. You use it to justify your own indecisiveness.
> *Turns back to him.*
What makes me so angry is that you've been using me as

79]

well. I do your work, fulfill your obligations . . . How can you say that's love? If anything, love is a giving and taking, an interchange of emotions, a gradual development based on physical attraction, complementary careers and simple social similarities.

HARRY. (*Clasps the back of the bench with one hand, presses the other to his cheek; indignantly*) So that's what you think!

ELLEN. That's precisely what I think!

HARRY. No romance, no tenderness, no subconscious . . . Love is *ooonly* a gradual development based on physical attraction, complementary careers and simple social similarities. That's *aaaall* it is.

ELLEN. Yes. That's *aaaall* it is.

HARRY. And you're not ashamed to say that to me?

ELLEN. Why should I be ashamed?

HARRY. Love is a gradual development based on physical attraction, complementary careers and simple social similarities!

ELLEN. That's right.

HARRY. (*Moves right to lamppost, turns back to* ELLEN) I can't get over it. My wife. My own wife. The woman who took the holy vows with me. You can stand there and look at me and say . . .

ELLEN. (*Curtly*) Love is a gradual development based on physical attraction, complementary careers and simple social similarities!

HARRY. Ellen, do what you want with me, curse me, step on me, tear me to pieces, but I beg you, out of consideration for all the days and nights we lived as man and wife, *do not say* . . .

ELLEN. (*Parrotlike*) Love is a gradual development based on physical attraction, complementary careers . . .

HARRY. (*Moves back to lamppost and cries out*) Ahhhhhh!
ELLEN *stops.* HARRY *moves left to front of bench.*
I do not believe that this is happening to us. Not to us. Not to Harry and Ellen Berlin.

ELLEN. It is happening to us. And you have to see it for what it is. It's not pleasant but there's no use pretending. There's something else you ought to know, then I'm done.
Turns away from him.
Harry . . . I'm in love with Milt Manville; and he loves me.
HARRY *freezes in absurd posture;* ELLEN *moves left, not noticing him.*
We both realize now that we acted too hastily. It's unfortunate that you came along when you did. I have no doubt that Milt and I would have mended our differences . . .
MILT *enters, right, wearing faded denim trousers which are too short and tight for him, a very large blue and white striped jersey that hangs over his trousers and a small black officer's jacket, without buttons or gold braid; his hair, which is still wet, lies flat on his scalp, and he has on a very small, white, sailor's cap. He is wearing sneakers without socks; he carries his clothes, still dripping, in a package tied by rope under his arm. Enraged, he storms by* HARRY *and paces back and forth center stage.*
Milt! What happened to you? Where were you?

MILT. Don't ask. Just don't ask. It was terrible.

ELLEN. But I . . .

MILT. I said don't ask!

ELLEN. (*Moves to* MILT) Why are you angry with me?

MILT. (*Glaring at* HARRY, *puts his bundle down on upstage bench*) He's at it again, huh? He tried to kill me, did you know that?

ELLEN. Harry?

MILT. Harry. Your husband. The one you were so worried about.

ELLEN. Oh, no.

MILT. Oh, yeah. He threw me off the bridge. Right over his shoulder. Lucky for me a barge was passing. They picked me up, gave me these clothes, a cup of coffee and a doughnut.
Shouting.
It was a cinnamon doughnut.

ELLEN. My poor Milt. You don't know how glad I am you're safe.

MILT. No thanks to you.

ELLEN. Milt! How can you say that?

MILT. Well, whose fault is it? I told you there was only one way out of this. It's him or us. One or the other. Ellen, sweetheart, it's not what you think.
Crosses down right to right of HARRY.
Look at him. He's no good to anyone, not even to himself.
ELLEN *follows and stands left of* HARRY; *both lean their elbows on his shoulders and examine him.*

We'd be doing him a favor. When you get down to it . . . What is it? Euthanasia. That's what it is. And remember what you said about euthanasia, hon?

ELLEN. They should be destroyed. Painlessly. By an impartial board of prominent citizens.

MILT. That's what you said. Well, isn't it the same as if we were on that board of prominent citizens? I mean, logically speaking.

ELLEN. There isn't much difference.

MILT. Of course not.

ELLEN. It's one of degree, not of kind.

MILT. Exactly.

> *Slight pause.*

I love you, El.

> As ELLEN *moves to* MILT, HARRY *slowly begins to fall left. They both catch him and hold him up.*

ELLEN. I love you, Milt.

MILT. For all eternity.

ELLEN. For ever and ever.

MILT. El.

ELLEN. I'm so nervous.

MILT. (*Takes her hand*) Don't be. Just look at my eyes, at me, sweetheart. Don't look at him and don't think about what you're doing. Just look at my eyes and say I love you, Milt Manville.

ELLEN. I love you, Milt Manville.

MILT. (*Facing* HARRY, *puts his arms around him, about his chest, and begins to pull him left*) I love you.

ELLEN. (*As* HARRY *gets past her, she bends down and picks up one leg in each hand and standing between them, helps* MILT *carry him up left to the alcove*) My Milton.

MILT. Ellen sweetheart.
>*They stare into each other's eyes.*

ELLEN. How I do love you . . .

MILT. Soon we'll be together. Always together.

ELLEN. My darling husband-to-be.
>*They carry* HARRY *to the right railing of the alcove,* ELLEN *having circled left, so that* MILT *is closest to the railing.* MILT *lays* HARRY's *still-rigid body on his stomach on the railing, while* ELLEN *puts his feet down on the ground.*

MILT. (*At railing*) Ellen, get him around . . .

ELLEN. (*Butts against* HARRY's *backside with her head in an attempt to push him over*) I love you, Milt Manville.
>*Repeats line again as she butts* HARRY.

MILT. (*In an effort to pull* HARRY *over,* MILT *puts one leg over railing straddling it, as he pulls at* HARRY. *However,* ELLEN *inadvertently pushes* HARRY *against* MILT, *throwing him off balance*) You're pushing me here . . .

ELLEN. I love you, Milt Manville. I love you, Milt Manville. Etc.

MILT. (*In attempt to regain balance, pulls other leg over railing. But* ELLEN *continues to push* HARRY *against him*) Ellen . . . For God's sake . . . You're pushing me, Ellen . . . Ellen . . .
>*MILT slips off the railing, screaming, with hands clutching empty air. Again a splash, and then a spray of water, which hits* HARRY *as it breaks over*

the railing. ELLEN *runs frantically to the railing right and peers over.* HARRY *suddenly comes to with a shudder of his head.*

ELLEN. Milt? Milt? Where are you? Are you there, Milt? Answer me! Oh, no, no, no . . .
> *Turning back from rail, begins to sob, wildly.*

HARRY. (*Now fully conscious, sees her, and goes to her*) Ellen, don't . . . I'm all right now. It was nothing.
> *Embraces her.*

You do love me. I knew you loved me. The birds, the sun, our sun . . .

ELLEN. Oh, stop it.
> *Pulls away from him.*

Milt. He fell over. He's down there!

HARRY. Milt?

ELLEN. He's drowning. Why don't you do something?

HARRY. (*Runs to left*) Help. Somebody. Help us!

ELLEN. (*Runs to right*) Help! Help!
> *Runs to left.*

HARRY. (*Running right*) Help us! Somebody!
> *Runs left to alcove and climbs up on railing right of alcove. Shouts.*

Milt, hold on, hold on!

ELLEN. (*Runs up right to railing left of* HARRY *and looks down*) Do you see him?

HARRY. There. That's him. He's getting into a rowboat. Where that light is.

ELLEN. (*Waving*) Milt! Milt!

HARRY. (*Shouting*) Hey, Milt! What the hell's wrong with you?

85]

LUV

ELLEN. He can't hear us.

HARRY. (*Still shouting*) You dumb bastard!

ELLEN. Thank God he's safe.
>   *Moves right, looks over railing.*
How do I get down . . . No. I'll wait here for him. He knows I'll be here.
>   *Sits on bench.*

HARRY. (*Gets down from railing*) I never thought he'd do anything as stupid as that.

ELLEN. He didn't . . . Oh, forget it.

HARRY. (*Goes to bench and lies down with head left and feet right in* ELLEN's *lap*) What a world. People trying to kill themselves, jumping off bridges, turning on gas, taking poison . . . They know; they feel it. The sky, look for yourself: it's been trying to rain all night but it can't do it, it can't, it's empty, like everything else, empty and dead. And soon . . .

ELLEN. (*Sharply; pushing him off bench.* HARRY *lands on hands and knees*) That's enough of that, Harry. Don't pretend you didn't hear me before. I told you Milt and I . . .

HARRY. (*Gets up, moves left*) You told me. All right. You told me. But why? What did I do wrong? Explain it to me. Give me a reason.

ELLEN. I've given you a dozen reasons. But if they won't do . . .
>   *Takes a small, rolled paper graph from her bag which is on the ground, right of the bench.*
Look. Look at this.
>   HARRY *sits left of her on bench, and she unrolls graph.*
These black vertical lines divide our four months of mar-

[86

riage into days. Now each time the red horizontal line hits the black vertical line that indicates one sexual experience over a twenty-four-hour period.

HARRY. Where's the red horizontal line?

ELLEN. There is none.
Rolls up graph.
Now do you understand?

HARRY. Why didn't you tell me? I'm trying to be a good husband, but if you don't tell me . . . I was never married before, you were, don't forget that!

ELLEN. You're supposed to know some things yourself.

HARRY. I was giving you time. I wanted us to become friends first . . . get to know one another, and then . . .
Gestures.
You should have told me. You definitely should have!

ELLEN. A lot of good that would have done.

HARRY. Why do you say that?

ELLEN. No normal man could have behaved the way you have these past four months. I'd rather not say any more.

HARRY. No, no, say it.
Crosses legs and leans back on bench.

ELLEN. It'll be painful.

HARRY. Say it. Go ahead.

ELLEN. Very well. I'll say it. You think you know yourself, Harry, but you don't know yourself at all. You never loved me. You're incapable of that kind of love. You loved . . . All this time . . . You loved . . . Milt.

HARRY. I . . . What?

ELLEN. Yes. Milt. Milt Manville. You always loved him, I

imagine. Even back at school. You married me as a substitute-figure because you couldn't confront him and your own latent homosexuality.

HARRY. What are you saying?

ELLEN. I'm saying you're queer, Harry.

HARRY. No, no, it can't be, I . . .

ELLEN. It can be and it is. All this explains your attitude toward life, your fits and
Holding up graph.
everything else. I am sorry but you asked for it.

HARRY. (*Incredulously*) I love Milt Manville.

ELLEN. I'm afraid you do, Harry.

HARRY. It's ridiculous. I don't even like the guy!

ELLEN. Don't you, Harry? The way he has of laughing, the way his lips curl up when he smiles . . .

HARRY. (*Open-faced*) His lips . . .

ELLEN. The way he carries himself, like a soldier, and when he's excited, his eyes, how they shine and sparkle . . .

HARRY. His eyes . . .

ELLEN. We both love him, Harry.

HARRY. (*Half convinced*) Milt.

ELLEN. (*Nodding*) Milt.

HARRY. (*Regretfully*) I never sent him flowers.

ELLEN. It's not an easy thing for someone to acknowledge.
Puts graph back into bag.

HARRY. His lips, his eyes . . . his legs . . .
Grimaces, expels a sound of repulsion.
No, no, you're crazy, Ellen. It's you I love, you!

[88

ELLEN *rises, moves away right.*
I'll show you. I'll prove it to you.

> *He throws her over his shoulder, runs about madly, indecisively, back and forth across bridge.*

ELLEN. (*Kicking, screaming*) Harry! Harry!

HARRY. I'll take you away. Someplace. Anyplace. You'll be happy! happy! I'll make you happy!

ELLEN. Put me down!

HARRY. We'll be happy! happy! We're going to be happy! happy!

ELLEN. Harry, will you put me . . .

HARRY. (*Lays her out on bench, smothers her with inept hugs*) Happy! Happy! Happy! Happy! You little honey-bunny, you . . . You mousy-wousy hot little flousy . . .

ELLEN. Don't! Stop it!

HARRY. (*Growling as he kisses and bites the nape of her neck*) Grrrr . . . Arrrr . . . Grrrrr . . .

ELLEN. (*Stamping her feet on bench*) Harry, no more, stop it now!

HARRY. (*Suddenly stops, gets up from her, and moves left*) *Confused.*
What's wrong? I'm trying to do what you told me.
> *Shouting.*
For cryin' out loud! Is there no satisfying a woman!

ELLEN. (*Sitting up*) Don't talk to me anymore . . . Just leave me alone and don't talk to me.

> MILT *enters down right, crosses to left, where he paces back and forth, even more enraged. He is wearing a very large pair of white bell-bottom trousers, a T-shirt, and a very small, ripped black*

wool sweater, sneakers, and a yellow southwester
oilskin cap.

ELLEN. (*Rises and crosses to him*) Milt!

MILT. (*Turning on her*) Don't talk to me.

ELLEN. What is . . .

MILT. I said don't talk to me!

HARRY. (*Moves to* ELLEN's *right; to* MILT) It's about time you
got here. I've been waiting . . .

MILT. Oh, shut up!

HARRY. Where's the five bucks . . .

MILT. (*Crosses right, in front of* HARRY; *sits center of bench*)
Did you hear me say shut up!

HARRY. Ellen, will you . . .

ELLEN. The same goes for me. Shut up!
Crosses right to bench; sits right of MILT.

HARRY *defiantly moves to bench, sits down left of*
MILT. *The three of them are now seated on the*
bench, grimly, stiffly, MILT *between the others,*
arms folded. A moment passes. HARRY *takes out*
a pad and pencil, begins to write a note. MILT
glances at him, and HARRY *turns so that he cannot*
read the note; then hands pencil and pad to
ELLEN, *carefully sneaking it over so that* MILT
cannot read what he has written. She, without
reading it, tears off note, crumples it and throws
it over her shoulder, writes a brief note to MILT,
passes pad and pencil to him. Without reading
it, he throws entire pad over his shoulder. He is
about to throw the pencil away as well, has second

thoughts, and begins to put it under his cap. HARRY
slaps his hand and pulls pencil away from him.

ELLEN. (*Quacking; not spoken*) Miltie? Miltie?

MILT. Don't bother me.

> HARRY *takes a small banana from his coat pocket*
> *and begins to peel it.*

ELLEN. (*Quacking each word*) Don't be angry with me.

MILT. Will you stop that stupid quacking.

ELLEN. Why is it my fault?

MILT. I asked you to do a simple lousy thing . . .

> HARRY *begins to eat the banana.*

ELLEN. I tried.

MILT. Not very hard, did you?

ELLEN. I did. Have pity. You're absolutely all I have.

MILT. (*Cynically*) I bet.

ELLEN. Would I be here otherwise, pleading with you like
this?

MILT. You still could be lying.

> HARRY *peels it down farther, and continues eating.*

ELLEN. (*Sticking her chin out*) Is this the face of a liar, Milt?
Is it?

MILT. (*He closely examines her face*) Why do I keep tortur-
ing myself! I'm not made of stone, El. You know me; you
know how I am.

ELLEN. Oh, Milt.

> *They kiss in a passionate embrace.* HARRY *watches;*
> *then takes final bite of banana, throws peel over*
> *his shoulder off the bridge, and pulls* MILT *away*
> *from* ELLEN.

HARRY. Hey, cut it out! That's my wife you're kissing there, buster!

MILT. Harry . . . for God's sake. Give us a break, will you?
Puts hand on HARRY's *knee.*

HARRY. (*Draws back, glances from corner of eye at* MILT's *hand; meaningfully*) Don't try anything funny.

MILT. What's that?
Puts his arm on top of bench around HARRY.

HARRY. (*Draws back even farther*) Just don't try anything funny. I love her. Her! Not you! Get that into your thick head!
Slight pause.
I can't help it.

MILT. (*Removes his arm*) I love her, too, Harry. And I can't help it. Why don't we . . . let her choose between us.

ELLEN. That's fair, Harry.

MILT. It's democratic.

HARRY. (*Hesitates, finally deciding, gets up.* MILT *gets up with him*) Ellen, my life, my . . .

ELLEN. (*Rises; abruptly*) I choose Milt Manville.
Taking her bag and MILT's *hand, she begins to move up left around the bench.*

MILT. (*Going with her*) Sorry, Harry.

HARRY. (*Moves up left above bench, grabs* ELLEN *and pulls her from* MILT) It's no good. I can't do it. I can't let you go. Don't ask.
ELLEN *ends up to the left of* HARRY.

ELLEN. (*Emphatically*) But, Harry, I don't love you.

HARRY. I don't give a damn whether you love me or not! I love you! I love you!
> *Placatingly.*

Ellen, you loved me once. You can love me again.

ELLEN. I'll never love you again, Harry. Now that I've lived with you I find you an utterly obnoxious person.

HARRY. All right, that's a beginning; that's a start.

ELLEN. (*Crosses right to upstage bench. Puts her bag down on bench*) What are we going to do, Milt?

MILT. (*Moves left to* HARRY) Harry, listen to me. Listen. I'm married to a woman at this very minute who has more things in common with you . . .

HARRY. Forget it. I'm not interested.

MILT. She reads, Harry, and she . . .

HARRY. I don't care if she belches Beethoven! I'm satisfied with Ellen.

MILT. Are you going to be able to keep an eye on her twenty-four hours a day? Because you're going to have to, Harry. The first chance we get we're checking into a hotel and it's not going to be to watch television, you can take my word on that!

HARRY. (*Moves right to* ELLEN) Ha! Ellen isn't the type to . . .

ELLEN. Don't count on that, Harry.

HARRY. You'd go with a man who's not your husband to some cheap sleezy hotel room that doesn't even have a television set!

ELLEN. (*Crosses left to* MILT) It would have a television set, wouldn't it, Milt?

>   *No response.*
> Milt?

MILT. (*Finally getting word out*) Of . . . of . . . of course!
>   *Forcefully.*
> It would be a first-class highly recommended A-1 hotel,
> with private bath, cocktail lounge, room service, breakfast
> in bed, everything!

ELLEN. (*Turns to* HARRY; *decisively*) I certainly would go to
> a first-class hotel with a man who's not my husband. And
> under the circumstances I would not consider it immoral.

HARRY. It's all a nightmare. A nightmare. None of it is real.
> You don't understand. If I lose Ellen, if I stop believing in
> love, I have nothing, nothing!
>   *Runs to railing to the right of alcove and jumps
>   up on it.*
> I might as well jump off the bridge right now!

MILT. (*Runs to him, grabs his legs*) Harry . . . you
> wouldn't . . . ?

ELLEN. (*Going to* MILT; *pulls him away*) He has no choice,
> Milt.

MILT. That's true.
>   *They both move downstage.*

ELLEN. If only I could have loved him more.

HARRY. I said, I might as well jump off this bridge right now.
> Doesn't anybody listen to me?

MILT. You tried, hon. Don't blame yourself. You were wonder-
> ful to him. I'm to blame for this. He was my best friend
> and I let him down.

ELLEN. You didn't, Milt. Don't even think it.

[94

HARRY. What's happening?
>   *Stares down at water below.*

MILT. I did my best. God knows I did my best.

ELLEN. You did. No friend would have done as much. I don't believe it.

HARRY. Hey!

MILT. There's no helping each other, is there?

ELLEN. We're all locked up in ourselves, in little separate compartments.

HARRY. Alone. All alone. No love. No hope. Nothing. Nothing. Aww, the hell with it.
>   *Takes white, woman's bathing cap out of pocket, puts it on.*

Let death come early. Yes. Yes. Let death come early.
>   *Holds nose; falls backward off bridge.*
>   *There is a splash. As MILT runs up to the railing to look over, a spray of water breaks over the railing and hits him. Soaking wet, he turns to ELLEN, and squirts out a mouthful of water.*

MILT. (*Moving to her*) El!

ELLEN. (*Embracing him*) Milt!

MILT. We're together.

ELLEN. At last. At long last.

MILT. My sweetheart.
>   *They kiss.*

ELLEN. We will have a baby, won't we?

MILT. Of course we will.

ELLEN. And we'll name him after Harry Berlin?

MILT. Harry Manville?

ELLEN. Harry Manville. I'm so happy, Milt.

MILT. Harry must be happy, too.

ELLEN. He is. I know he is.

MILT. I love you, sweetheart.
> *Kisses her and sweeps her up in his arms. Carries her to scooter as he hums the "Wedding March." She laughs, joins in. He puts her down, and goes to the scooter.*

ELLEN. I love you, my darling first-and-only husband.

MILT. (*Taking scooter off stand*) Not as much as I love you. Never. Never.

ELLEN. More than you love me.

MILT. (*Turns to* ELLEN) You couldn't love me more than I love you.

ELLEN. Much, much, much more.

MILT. (*Slight pause*) How much more?
> *Starts the scooter, gets on.*

ELLEN. (*Apprehensively*) Milt . . .

MILT. That's a reasonable question.

ELLEN. (*Gets on scooter behind* MILT) Don't start.

MILT. Just how much more?

ELLEN. Please, Milt.

MILT. (*Beginning to drive off right*) No, no . . . Never mind "please Milt." What about Harry?

ELLEN. What about Linda?

MILT. I never loved Linda.
> *They are disappearing offstage.*

ELLEN. But, you slept with Linda, didn't you? Didn't you? Didn't you . . . ?

> *As they exit,* HARRY *appears and begins to climb over the railing. He has lost his overcoat, is soaking wet, and is draped in seaweed. As he gets over the railing, he yells after* MILT.

HARRY. Milt! Milt! Where the hell are you going? Ellen, bring him back . . . Where's my five bucks, you cheap bastard!

> *Suddenly a dog dashes onstage from off right.* HARRY *sees it, howls with terror, begins to run left. The dog catches him and begins to pull at his pants leg.* HARRY *runs about in a circle trying to dislodge him, and finally in desperation runs to the lamppost, leaps, and hangs on to the crossbar. He hangs there, with the dog clinging to his pants leg.*

CURTAIN